T0339920

Precious

Examining how the discourses of youth, race, poverty and identity take shape when *Push* is adapted to the big screen, this book brings together valuable research to delve into representations of African-American girlhood.

The book draws attention to how Black girlhood takes shape in the film under the dominant White discourses that racialise non-White bodies, and examines how these discourses inform a critical reception of the film and Precious, as a Black girl. Through a consideration of Black culture and heritage, it questions what narratives of girlhood, growth and development are afforded to the main character, in a film that is informed by neoliberal and colour-blind discourses. Highlighting the social context in which *Precious* was received, the book draws attention to how a discussion of *Precious* in the critical press gives insight into the racial politics that were dominant at the time of the film's release. It considers whether race impacts how the film engages with, reflects and moves beyond conventions within the genre of youth film.

Concise and engaging, this vital book sheds light on underrepresented areas of film studies that make it an invaluable resource for students and scholars of film, race and youth cultures.

Katherine Whitehurst is a lecturer in media and film at the University of Liverpool. Her research centres on adaptation; fairy tales; child, youth and age studies; screen and literature; girlhood and identity; cultural memory; feminism; and gender.

Cinema and Youth Cultures
Series Editors: Siân Lincoln and Yannis Tzioumakis

Cinema and Youth Cultures engages with well-known youth films from American cinema as well the cinemas of other countries. Using a variety of methodological and critical approaches the series volumes provide informed accounts of how young people have been represented in film, while also exploring the ways in which young people engage with films made for and about them. In doing this, the Cinema and Youth Cultures series contributes to important and long-standing debates about youth cultures, how these are mobilized and articulated in influential film texts and the impact that these texts have had on popular culture at large.

The Beatles and Film
From Youth Culture to Counterculture
Stephen Glynn

Clerks
'Over the Counter' Culture and Youth Cinema
Peter Templeton

Moonlight
Screening Black Queer Youth
Maria Flood

The Commitments
Youth, Music, and Authenticity in 1990s Ireland
Nessa Johnston

Precious
Identity, Adaptation and the African-American Youth Film
Katherine Whitehurst

For more information about this series, please visit: www.routledge.com/Cinema-and-Youth-Cultures/book-series/CYC

Precious

Identity, Adaptation and the African-American Youth Film

Katherine Whitehurst

"You Feel You've Witnessed Nothing Less Than the Birth of a Soul."

Mo'Nique

Paula Patton

Mariah Carey

Lenny Kravitz

Gabourey Sidibe

p r e c i o u s

Routledge
Taylor & Francis Group

LONDON AND NEW YORK

First published 2022
by Routledge
4 Park Square, Milton Park, Abingdon, Oxon OX14 4RN

and by Routledge
605 Third Avenue, New York, NY 10158

Routledge is an imprint of the Taylor & Francis Group, an informa business

© 2022 Katherine Whitehurst

The right of Katherine Whitehurst to be identified as author of this work has been asserted in accordance with sections 77 and 78 of the Copyright, Designs and Patents Act 1988.

British Library Cataloguing-in-Publication Data
A catalogue record for this book is available from the British Library

Library of Congress Cataloging-in-Publication Data
Names: Whitehurst, Katherine, author.
Title: Precious : identity, adaptation and the African-American youth film / Katherine Whitehurst.
Description: Abingdon, Oxon ; New York : Routledge, 2022. | Series: Cinema and youth cultures | Includes bibliographical references and index.
Identifiers: LCCN 2021043629 (print) | LCCN 2021043630 (ebook) | ISBN 9781138681859 (hardback) | ISBN 9781032209487 (paperback) | ISBN 9781315545547 (ebook)
Subjects: LCSH: Precious (Motion picture) | African Americans in motion pictures. | Girls in motion pictures.
Classification: LCC PN1997.2.P733 2022 (print) | LCC PN1997.2.P733 2022 (ebook) | DDC 791.45/72—dc23/eng/20211013
LC record available at https://lccn.loc.gov/2021043629
LC ebook record available at https://lccn.loc.gov/2021043630

ISBN: 978-1-138-68185-9 (hbk)
ISBN: 978-1-032-20948-7 (pbk)
ISBN: 978-1-315-54554-7 (ebk)

DOI: 10.4324/9781315545547

Typeset in Times New Roman
by Apex CoVantage, LLC

Frontispiece: *Precious*: based on the novel *Push* by Sapphire. Courtesy Lee Daniels/Kobal/Shutterstock

Contents

Figures

Series editors' introduction

Despite the high visibility of youth films in the global media marketplace, especially since the 1980s when Conglomerate Hollywood realised that such films were not only strong box office performers but also the starting point for ancillary sales in other media markets as well as for franchise building, academic studies that focused specifically on such films were slow to materialise. Arguably, the most important factor behind academia's reluctance to engage with youth films was a (then) widespread perception within the Film and Media Studies communities that such films held little cultural value and significance, and therefore were not worthy of serious scholarly research and examination. Just like the young subjects they represented, whose interests and cultural practices have been routinely deemed transitional and transitory, so were the films that represented them perceived as fleeting and easily digestible, destined to be forgotten quickly, as soon as the next youth film arrived in cinema screens a week later.

Under these circumstances, and despite a small number of pioneering studies in the 1980s and early 1990s, the field of 'youth film studies' did not really start blossoming and attracting significant scholarly attention until the 2000s and in combination with similar developments in cognate areas such as 'girl studies'. However, because of the paucity of material in the previous decades, the majority of these new studies in the 2000s focused primarily on charting the field and therefore steered clear of long, in-depth examinations of youth films or was exemplified by edited collections that chose particular films to highlight certain issues to the detriment of others. In other words, despite providing often wonderfully rich accounts of youth cultures as these have been captured by key films, these studies could not have possibly dedicated sufficient space to engage with more than just a few key aspects of youth films.

In more recent (post-2010) years, a number of academic studies started delimiting their focus and therefore providing more space for in-depth examinations of key types of youth films, such as slasher films and biker films or examining youth films in particular historical periods. From that point on, it was a matter of time for the first publications that focused exclusively on key youth films from a number of perspectives to appear (*Mamma Mia! The Movie*, *Twilight* and *Dirty Dancing* are among the first films to receive this treatment). Conceived primarily as edited collections, these studies provided a multifaceted analysis of these films, focusing on such issues as the politics of representing youth, the stylistic and narrative choices that characterise these films and the extent to which they are representative of a youth cinema, the ways these films address their audiences, the ways youth audiences engage with these films, the films' industrial location and other relevant issues.

It is within this increasingly maturing and expanding academic environment that the Cinema and Youth Cultures volumes arrive, aiming to consolidate existing knowledge, provide new perspectives, apply innovative methodological approaches, offer sustained and in-depth analyses of key films and therefore become the 'go to' resource for students and scholars interested in theoretically informed, authoritative accounts of youth cultures in film. As editors, we have tried to be as inclusive as possible in our selection of key examples of youth films by commissioning volumes on films that span the history of cinema, including the silent film era; that portray contemporary youth cultures as well as ones associated with particular historical periods; that represent examples of mainstream and independent cinema; that originate in American cinema and the cinemas of other nations; that attracted significant critical attention and commercial success during their initial release and that were 'rediscovered' after an unpromising initial critical reception. Together these volumes are going to advance youth film studies while also being able to offer extremely detailed examinations of films that are now considered significant contributions to cinema and our cultural life more broadly.

We hope readers will enjoy the series.

Siân Lincoln & Yannis Tzioumakis
Cinema & Youth Cultures Series Editors

Acknowledgements

I would like to thank Yannis for his patience, kindness and support throughout the writing of this book. Your feedback has been invaluable.

To my dad, thank you for spending so much time reflecting on your childhood memories with me and for giving me your feedback on the book's introduction. I have learned so much from you over the years and I feel blessed to have you as my dad.

Finally, to my husband Lorcan who is the love of my life and my rock. I couldn't imagine life without you. Thank you for always supporting me in my goals and ambitions.

Precious
An introduction

As the title of the film would suggest, *Precious: Based on the Novel Push by Sapphire* (Daniels, 2009; here on referred to as *Precious*) is an adaptation of the Black, Afrocentric, feminist poet Sapphire's 1996 book titled *Push*. The book, which scholars have referred to as a neo-slave narrative (Michlin 2006, McNeil 2012), explores the politics of race, poverty, the body and gender in America through the eyes and experiences of Claireece Precious Jones (referred to as Precious; played by Gabourey Sidibe), an obese, poor, HIV-positive, 16-year-old African-American girl who is the mother of two children, one of which who has Down's syndrome. As various critics have commented (Edelstein 2009, Stapleton 2004), the book is difficult to read. It details Precious' experiences of rape, as well as her experiences of terrible physical and verbal abuse at the hands of her father, Carl (Rodney Jackson), and mother, Mary (Mo'Nique). While Precious' story is about her struggle to escape her abusive home life and past, it is also a story about the various social systems (educational, medical, child protection, policing and welfare services) that fail to help the young protagonist when she is in need.

The book examines the prejudices that Precious comes up against as she tries to build a life and future for herself. It also details the prejudices Precious holds and how she learns to question and challenge her own beliefs and values. As McNeil (2012: 16) asserts, the book, through Precious, articulates how the mind can be decolonised and how through developing one's social awareness, one can exist in the world in a different way. This coming-of-age narrative depicts Precious' journey as she discovers her own voice, but it does not provide the audience with the happy ending they might hope for and would expect from a coming-of-age story. Instead, her HIV-positive diagnosis, an infection she contracts from her father in the late 1980s (1987 to be precise), means that her future is foreclosed before it ever really begins.[1] Precious' story is nonetheless more hopeful than what many youths have experienced and continue to live through, as the trailer for Michael Leoni's recently released film, *American Street Kid* (Leoni,

DOI: 10.4324/9781315545547-1

2020), demonstrates.[2] Precious is given shelter, she forms friendships and a support system, she is able to feed both herself and her children, and she finally escapes her abusive home life. Nonetheless, these are small mercies in an otherwise dark book.

It is this narrative that the film adapts. Directed by Lee Daniels, *Precious* has been described by critics as at times depressing, harrowing or challenging in its subject matter (Koch 2009, Rainer 2009, Biancolli 2009), as 'hit[ting] you in the gut' (Hammond 2009: 37) and as 'not always easy to watch' (Lumenick 2009). On the other hand, it is also in many ways more playful in its use of fantasy and escapism than Sapphire's novel, leading some critics to describe its tone as camp, in terms of both its imagery and its soundtrack (Gilbey 2010). Specifically, the film tones down the depictions of (sexual) violence and provides more detailed moments of escapism that are vibrant and pull the viewer away from Precious' otherwise dark life. The film visually situates itself in the 1980s by making use of fashion, settings and décor that are recognisable from the era. However, as one might expect of a film produced in more contemporary times, it is the racial dimensions of those times (the late 2000s) that inform the film's politics, as I will discuss further in Chapter 4. As such, while the film is at all times haunted by the novel, it does not simply replicate its text.

Daniels struggled for 8 years to get the rights to the novel, as Sapphire was resistant to having the book adapted for the big screen (Lerner and Lerner 2009). After Daniels produced the films *Monster's Ball* (Forster, 2001), *The Woodsman* (Kassell, 2004) and *Shadowboxer* (Daniels, 2005), he re-approached Sapphire to request the rights to *Push*. This time he was successful (Longwell 2009: 8). After signing away the rights to her book, Sapphire did not expect to have any part in the making of the film. However, she admitted that Daniels repeatedly contacted her to ensure that the adaptation reflected the essence of her novel (Knopfdoubleday 2009). While, as will be explored in Chapter 1, the book and film do diverge from one another, sometimes in quite significant ways, this reverence to the original can be seen clearly in Daniels' adaptation, as the film directly incorporates lines and scenes from the book.

Getting the rights to Sapphire's book was not the only hurdle Daniels had to cross to produce the film. According to the filmmaker, when making his past films he struggled to get funding from Hollywood (Longwell 2009: 9). In this respect, when it came to *Precious*, because of his past difficulties and the film's subject matter, Daniels decided to bypass traditional funding routes to finance the film (Schuker 2009). He sought out an independent donor and ultimately obtained financing from Sarah Siegel-Magness and Gary Magness (ibid.). After the film was produced, it was screened at various film festivals, such as Sundance and Cannes, where it attracted the support of Oprah

Winfrey and Tyler Perry (UrbanBridgez E-Zine 2009) and received attention from both Lionsgate and The Weinstein Company (Longwell 2009: 8). While Lionsgate ultimately secured the rights to distribute the film, The Weinstein Company contested this ownership and claimed that it had the right to distribute *Precious* itself (Belloni 2010: 5, Longwell 2009: 8). The matter was settled in court, and it was found that The Weinstein Company had failed to finalise their deal before the rights were sold to Lionsgate (Belloni 2010: 5).

Both the book and the film received a mixed reception. On the one hand, these texts have been praised for giving a voice to a section of society that is rarely ever heard or depicted. As Griffin asserts, 'Precious is easily read as sympathetic towards Black womanhood' (2014: 183) and as Liddell agrees, sexual abuse survivors are rarely given voice within 'Black sociological, psychological, or imaginative literature' (1999: 137). On the other hand, members of the African-American community were critical of both texts for reaffirming racist stereotypes, such as the Welfare Queen and violent Black male sexuality (or more simply the Black man as rapist) (Kelley 2009: 61, Jarman 2012: 163, 166–7 & 173, McNeil 2012: 14, David 2016: 176, Liddell 1999: 145).

Sapphire's work is in part a response to the 1996 welfare reforms in the U.S. that saw single Black mothers being deprived of the support they needed to escape poverty (Michlin 2006). Her portrayal of Precious' struggle to rise above her situation as a single mother and the way the welfare system seemed to work against her goals for self-improvement are where Sapphire's political criticisms of the system can most clearly be seen. However, in contrast with this depiction, her representation of Mary as a welfare cheat mirrors some of the stereotypes that are routinely applied to Black women. Furthermore, as Carl is the only African-American man in the book, the text reaffirms the stereotype of Black man as rapist, by providing no other representations of African-American masculinity that could challenge this myth. The film similarly makes use of these stereotypes and, while it is not as damning of Black masculinity as the book, in adapting this narrative it also replicates the depiction of the Black man as rapist. Furthermore, the film, which lacks some of the political and feminist nuance found in the book, has been accused of being another 'media product . . . about Black suffering made mainly for the White gaze' (Kyrölä 2017: 260; see also Griffin 2014). In addition to these criticisms, as McNeil notes, as 'incest in black communities [is] a traditionally taboo subject in African-American literature since it undermined black "nation building"' (2012: 12), it is perhaps not surprising that both these texts were not warmly received by sections of the Black community.

As my analysis of the book and film will highlight, both texts draw on racist stereotypes of Black sexuality, masculinity and poverty that have long haunted the African-American community. However, to label either text as simply stereotypical undermines and erases the progressive political and social work at play in them. This book will neither seek to dismiss these works for their, at times, regressive social framings nor will it seek to singularly celebrate them for giving voice to the often-voiceless poor African-American girl. Instead, I seek to unpack how both texts, though primarily the film, work within stereotypical framings of the Black community and broader understandings of Black girlhood to shed light on the social politics that inform them.

In many ways, the public reaction to the film, with primarily White Western critics celebrating the work, and members of the Black community questioning, if not criticising, it, reflects the film's political positioning between the expectations and hopes of White and Black communities. As will become apparent, much of my consideration of this film and its representation of Black girlhood focuses on how the narrativisation of the latter is held in relation to White Western middle-class understandings of girlhood as well as Black feminist understandings of Black femininity. In so doing, this book highlights how many of the dominant frameworks used to understand and evaluate youth fail to find resonance with the depiction of Black girlhood that Daniels provides. Through an examination of this discord, this book aims to reveal the space that this film carved out for Black girlhood, and to question how such narratives were understood within critical responses to the film.

My own positioning and reading as an academic seeking to make sense of this film and its engagement with Black girlhood is itself divided between different racial frameworks. As a White, middle-class, Canadian woman, my experiences of race and racism are a world away from the realities that Precious faces. As a White female, I have had, for all of my life, the luxury of not having to see my own colour. Growing up I was never asked by my society to question how the colour of my skin, and my blindness of its colour, gave me social, economic and systemic benefits at the expense of others. As Canada often prides itself on its inclusivity, discourses of multiculturalism often cover over or shut down discussions of racism and structural racism in my country, though they are certainly both alive and well within Canada's borders. One only needs to look at the poor and criminal treatment of the aboriginal community to see that this is the case.

While in my late teen and adult years I became more conscious of my own privilege and how this privilege perpetuates the repression of others, I was not ignorant of race and racism growing up. My father is an American from a Southern state, Virginia, with an extended family from North Carolina and Alabama. He commonly recounted stories about race relations in the Hampton Roads area of Virginia where he grew up, including what it was like when schools were de-segregated, how he grew up with an African-American nanny and housekeeper who minded him when his parents were working, and how, as a boy, his nanny would call him her 'little Kennedy'. This nickname, while a play on his name 'Ken', seemed not simply to be because she doted on him, but because she expected him to live up to the hope of reform that Kennedy promised the Black community.

In some ways, his stories are from another lifetime, and yet I also knew that the racism and race dynamics he witnessed continued. I can still remember visiting a great aunt in the late 1990s who lived in a town in North Carolina that was divided. The barber in this town warned my brother and me not to cross the main street. He said that there were dangerous Black people on the other side. Having spent most of the morning on that side of the street without experiencing any level of hostility, I could not understand who these 'dangerous Black people' were. In the midst of this confusion, I became uncomfortable and frightened when this barber showed us a gun he had in a drawer. It is my recollection that he told me that he would use it on any Black person that threatened his shop, though admittedly as I was a child, my memory of this assertion may be inaccurate or informed by years of reflection. Nonetheless, I do remember that I did not cross the street again, but not because I was afraid of Black people. So I felt I knew what racism was, even though I had not been explicitly discriminated against because of my race and even though I was not confronted with this type of overt and pervasive racism where I lived in Canada. At the time, racism to me was primarily an irrational hate expressed by one person against another because of their race. I did not yet understand that racism was also systemic and that as a member of my society, I was drawn into it by circumstance, no matter how passively or unconsciously it was done.

Since my childhood, my father has complicated this exchange with the barber for me through his own memories. Unbeknown to me, the barber had been robbed at knifepoint in the shop. While he did not directly tell my father that the crime was committed by Black people in the community, my father said it was strongly implied to him that it was. Apparently, the gun he kept was not loaded and the man was not a strong gun advocate; he was simply afraid and using the gun as a visible deterrent. His warnings to us, while shaped clearly by a racist discourse, was, as my father highlighted, a quick reference point for taking caution in a community, that as outsiders, my brother and I knew nothing about. All this is not to say that the man's engage-ment with me and my brother was not shaped by racism. Both my father and I would agree that it was. What it highlights is that my understanding of the race dynamics in that town were, and in many ways continue to be, underde-veloped. I think I will always struggle to make sense of the dynamics within that town. After all, at the time of my grandmother's funeral, friends of my great aunt's from within the town's African-American community brought food and great sympathy to her house. I can still remember the mountains of food that lined her table and which was given by everyone in that community with such generosity, regardless of race.

All of this is to say, that while I am conscious of many of the politics surrounding race, my experience of race and racism has always and will always be shaped by my relatively privileged position as a White Canadian female. As such, my reading of *Precious* and the film's representations of race in America will inevitably be shaped by this positioning. This caveat is not intended to excuse my reading of the film nor is it intended to ask for the reader's leniency. Rather, it is intended to provide the reader with further context so they might have a clear framework in which to judge my findings and to understand how my conclusions have been reached.

In some ways writing this book was a dilemma. Much of my previous research centres around *bildungsroman* and *reifungsroman* narratives about White Western girls and women, though the racial dimensions of Whiteness are not explored in this early work, which is instead framed by a consideration of age politics. As much of my writing and the writing in youth studies more generally makes use of White Western theories and frameworks, the opportunity to write on *Precious* was a chance to widen my understanding of girlhood through the lens of race, something I have wanted but have been hesitant to do, rightly or wrongly, because of my privileged position as a White woman.

At all times I have felt like an outsider to this film, the community it depicts and the Black feminist scholarship and ideas that it adapts. Even my reading of the film seems to be at odds with some members of the Black community. For example, Daniels describes the humour in his film and how he was laughing when neighbourhood bullies pushed Precious to the ground (Pride 2009). Initially, I was surprised by this assertion as I did not find the scene funny, nor could I think of any funny moments in the film. I dismissed this discord through an assumption that Daniels' claims were not reflected in the film he actually produced, regardless of his intentions. However, after reading Crawford's (2012) account of how her students who were multi-racial and from the inner city read some of the scenes of abuse as comedic, I understood that no matter how sympathetic a reading I tried to provide of the film, my subject position would always keep me outside the community depicted.

I have consequently sought to embrace this outsider position to question my own readings of Sapphire's book and Daniels' film in relation to what race scholars have said about the film, the novel and about race relations in America more broadly. As systemic racism and White privilege often rely on the invisible status of Whiteness, reflecting on Dyer's (1997) consideration of Whiteness, this book draws attention to how Black girlhood takes shape in the film under the dominance of the universal human constructed within

White Western discourses, and examines how these discourses inform a critical reception of the film and Precious, as a Black girl. This consideration of Whiteness will not usurp a consideration of Black culture, representation and politics. Instead, it is intended to reflect the way that race relations in America are shaped and informed by the dominant White discourses that racialise non-White bodies. In this way, this book follows Griffin's 'commitment to intersectionality' aiming to examine 'how whiteness is privileged in *Precious* at the intersection of race, gender and class' (2014: 183).

Chapter 1 focuses on how *Precious* takes shape as an adaptation. Staying clear of debates surrounding fidelity, the chapter details when and how the book and movie align and diverge to illustrate the ideological and political questions at the heart of each text. By unpacking how violence is illustrated within these works, the chapter investigates how issues such as rape, incest, racism and disease take shape in them. As one might expect, as these two texts are shaped by different historical moments, author/auteur, and media constraints and possibilities, the ideas and values that are narrated vary considerably between each text. The chapter argues that while the book endeavours to explore the politics of race and to understand social issues that extend beyond the poor African-American household, the film erases these other voices and positionings, and more firmly roots the narrative within the African-American community (despite the director's claims to the contrary; UrbanBridgez E-Zine 2009). In illustrating the different landscapes of these works and by unpacking their political frameworks, this chapter serves as a basis to understand the film as a text worthy of investigation in its own right. It gives further clarification to the political dimensions of the film with the intention of creating a contextual base in which the remaining three chapters are built.

Chapter 2 situates *Precious* within the broader genre of youth film. It questions how the frameworks and conventions of this genre give insight into how African-American girlhood and African-American coming-of-age narratives align with and deviate from broader understandings of youth culture texts, which are often read and understood within a White Western framework. I consider how *Precious'* alignment with the high-school film subgenre sees the film engage with stock characters, particularly the saviour teacher. I investigate how the intersection of the saviour teacher and the film's colour tone racism facilitates the promotion of White middle-class values at the expense of an impoverished African-American community. The chapter also considers how the romantic elements often found in youth films are racialised within *Precious*. Through a consideration of Precious' romantic imaginings and her sexual abuse and harassment, the chapter argues that the dark Black male body is framed as a deviant and threatening body, and consequently excluded from the romance narrative. In line with this consideration, the chapter questions whether the film closes down possible romantic narratives for the main character as it limits her romantic engagements to fantasy. Finally, as the institutionalisation of adolescence is an important feature of the youth film, the chapter concludes by outlining how the institutions of the home, the school and the state are negotiated by Precious, and how these institutions in turn inform the shape and development of her girlhood.

Picking up on the insights on girlhood and genre discussed in Chapter 2, Chapter 3 investigates how African-American girlhood and the dominant Western discourses surrounding the age-based categories of child, adolescent and adult shape and inform Precious' coming-of-age narrative. The chapter considers how the historical framing of African-American children as nonchildren, as described by Olson (2017: 23), disrupts White Western discourses centred around coming-of-age. The chapter begins by analysing how the child is depicted within the film. It argues that as the Black child is framed as nonchild, the Black child is divorced from the narratives of childhood innocence that usually haunts dominant Western understandings of that particular age category. Following that, the chapter outlines how broader stereotypical framings of the African-American community are applied to the Black child. It suggests that this alignment sees the distance between childhood and adulthood closed. Centrally, this chapter argues that as the life stages of childhood, adolescence and adulthood become blurred, the linear framework of the coming-of-age narrative is problematised within the film and with it the future potential of the child is limited and undermined.

The final chapter moves away from earlier discussions of narrative to unpack the political landscape that informed the film's critical reception. The core argument is that critical reviews of the movie give insight into the colour-blind politics that were dominant at the time of its release. The chapter investigates the racism that was often at the heart of the critical press' engagement with and promotion of Precious. In line with this consideration, it questions how and whether reviews highlighted the African-American community's reception of the film, and contemplates the dynamics of race relations at the time of the film's release. Finally, this chapter illustrates how a discussion of the racial dimensions of Hollywood became entwined within or evaded critical reviews of Precious and, in so doing, demonstrates how the racial exclusion of Black culture and narratives become rationalised in the wake of the film's success.

The book concludes by detailing how the film is situated in relation to the broader catalogue of films about African-American girlhood. I begin by briefly considering the similarities between Precious and films that were released alongside it, before I account for the films about African-American girlhood that have been released since 2009. I question whether these films have greatly evolved from the narratives and framings found in *Precious*, before highlighting the areas for future research that these films point towards.

Notes

1 In the sequel to *Push*, *The Kid* (2011), Precious dies of the disease. Despite the early efforts to raise her son in a supportive and loving environment, after her death her son is left to the care of the state, where he is put in foster homes and a catholic orphanage where he is sexually abused. The book follows his traumatic transition from childhood to adulthood after the death of his mother. Unlike Precious, her son is not just a victim but also a perpetrator of violence. In this way, the sequel explores how abuse and victimhood can lead to further violence and dysfunctional behaviour.

2 In this film the lives of homeless youths are explored. Many of these youths give accounts of the abuse, physical, emotional and sexual, that they experienced at home. However, while their experiences of abuse find resonance with the experiences of abuse depicted in *Precious* and *Push*, unlike Precious, who is saved by education and who eventually finds some level of safety and security through the support of social services and welfare programmes, many of the teens depicted in this film struggle to get this kind of help and support. Instead, they have often been left to face the dangers of the streets where violence, rape, drug abuse and death become a part of their everyday lives.

1 Adapting *Push* to *Precious*

In this chapter, I examine the relationship between the book *Push* and the film *Precious*. In line with contemporary writings on adaptation theory, I outline what is at the core of these texts, to detail how the film and the book each seek to articulate the story. In so doing, I do not make arguments about the need for fidelity, in so far as I do not argue for the value of the original over the adaptation, or vice versa. As many adaptation scholars (Geraghty 2008, Hutcheon 2006, Cartmell and Whelehan 1999, McFarlane 1996, to name a few) have noted, these are subjective arguments that limit rather than advance the critical analysis of adapted texts. Instead, by investigating how these texts align with and differ from each other, I highlight the discourses each text mobilises and values they express. As McCallum notes, when adaptation and preceding text align they can often serve to 'affirm and reinforce cultural assumptions associated with the pretext' and can thus fortify 'values and ideas that a society sees as having cultural worth' (2021: 2). Yet, as adaptations also adapt a pretext they often do so 'in the light of contemporary and local issues and concerns' (ibid). Adaptations can consequently serve to uphold, challenge, reimagine or introduce discourses and ideologies that are reflective of the society and period the adaptation was produced in. My consideration of *Precious*' fidelity to and adaptation of *Push* will thus unpack the ideologies and discourses both works do and do not share.

As *Precious* is a transmedial adaptation, I at times consider how the medial differences between the book and the film facilitate particular readings of each text's content. I will not, however, seek to engage with broader media specificity debates to make claims about the possibilities for storytelling that each medium affords (as discussed by Gaudreault and Marion 2004, Maras and Sutton 2000, Carroll 1985). Instead, where I account for medial differences, I use this consideration to unpack the ideological framings of each work. Before beginning the work described previously, I will outline the definition of adaptation this chapter will use and then illustrate how *Precious* might be understood and read as an adaptation within this framework.

DOI: 10.4324/9781315545547-2

Scholars have long debated how to define adaptation. In 1984, Andrew

> assumed that [as] the task of adaptation is the reproduction . . . of some-
> thing essential about an original text[,] . . . [a]daptation . . . become[s]
> a matter of searching two systems of communication for elements of
> equivalent position in the systems.
>
> (423–5)

This early understanding of adaptation saw it defined around ideas of translation and replication. However, these arguments were soon problematised by scholars who questioned whether equivalency could be found when different conventions shape and inform different media (see Geraghty 2008, Hutcheon 2006, Cartmell and Whelehan 1999, McFarlane 1996, Mitry 1971). This approach to defining adaptation was further critiqued for its privileging of the source text. Scholars who recognised adaptation as a product as well as a process sought to 'destabilize . . . the tendency to believe that the origin text is of primary importance' (Whelehan 1999: 3) when defining an adaptation. To question the importance of the primary source, scholars considered well-known texts that audiences would be familiar with 'regardless of whether they'd ever actually read [the texts on which they were based]' (3–4); they challenged the idea that texts have an 'extractable "essence"' (Stam 2000: 57); or they examined adaptation as a process of reception (Grant 2002, Geraghty 2008). By moving the discussion away from issues of fidelity, scholars sought to consider adaptations as texts with their own aura and to make claims for analysing an adaptation as a text in its own right.

Hutcheon, returning to the idea that adaptation is a process of repetition, similarly sought to move the discussion of adaptation away from arguments about fidelity by highlighting that adaptation was a process of 'repetition without replication' (2006: 7). Perceiving adaptation as a process and a product, she defines it 'from three distinct but interrelated perspectives' (ibid). Firstly, she explores adaptation as a 'formal entity or product' that is 'announced' and provides an 'extensive transposition of a particular work or works' (ibid). She states that:

> [t]his "transcoding" can involve a shift of medium (a poem to a film) or
> genre (an epic to a novel), . . . a change of frame and therefore context
> [. . . or] a shift in ontology from the real to the fictional.
>
> (7–8)

Secondly, she considers adaptation as a process of creation as the artist (re-) interprets and (re-)creates a work. Finally, she investigates adaptation as a process of reception. She concludes that 'adaptation is a form of intertextuality: we experience adaptations (*as adaptations*) as palimpsests through our memory of other works that resonate through repetition with variation' (8).

In addition to creating a flexible definition for adaptation, Hutcheon importantly connects scholars who see adaptations as containing a shared core and those who define adaptation based on their broader intertextual nature. Reflecting the former, McFarlane states that 'narrative, at certain levels, is undeniably not only the chief factor novels and the films based on them have in common but is the chief transferable element' (1996: 12). According to McFarlane, the adaptation becomes differentiated from texts it shares a core with 'by means of different plot strategies which alter sequence, highlight different emphases, which – in a word – defamiliarize the story' (23). For McFarlane, the core serves an important function in the process of adaptation as the adaptation seemingly derives from the process of transferring a core and adapting 'aspects of [a story's] enunciation' (21).

McFarlane's arguments, which were not universally accepted by scholars, were particularly challenged by Stam's consideration of adaptations as intertextual texts. Stam denied that there was 'an extractable "essence," a kind of heart of the artichoke hidden "underneath" the surface details of style', arguing instead that 'a single novelistic text comprises a series of verbal signals that can generate a plethora of possible readings, including even readings of the narrative itself' (2000: 57). Stam's rejection of a core sees him extend the definition of adaptation to all texts that are intertextual, with 'every text form[ing] an intersection of textual surfaces' as they participate in an ongoing dialogue with the texts that surround them (64).

Stam's approach proved popular as it enabled scholars to further distance a consideration of adaptation from discussions of fidelity (Leitch 2017: 5). Yet his inclusivity is in many ways problematic. As Geraghty (2008: 4) highlights, in extending the definition of adaptation, the boundaries of what is or is not an adaptation can become blurred. Negotiating McFarlane's and Stam's perspectives, Hutcheon asserts that '[t]o deal with adaptations is to think of them as . . . inherently "palimpsestuous" works, haunted at all times by their adapted texts' (2006: 6), and argues that adaptations bring 'our intertextual expectations about medium and genre, as well as about [a] specific work, . . . to the forefront of our attention' (22). Yet while Hutcheon acknowledges the intertextual nature of adaptation, she provides boundaries for this intertextuality by defining it as an 'extended intertextual engagement' (8). In this way, the intertextual elements that make an adaptation identifiable as an adaptation are not based on fleeting reference but on the sustained allusion to a preceding work or works. As part of this extended intertextual engagement, Hutcheon identifies the main component that links adapted and preceding text(s). She states:

Most theories of adaptation assume, however, that the story is the common denominator, the core of what is transposed across different media and genres, each of which deals with the story in formally different ways and I would add, through different modes of engagement – narrating, performing, or interacting.

(10)

For Hutcheon, while texts may share a variety of elements during this extended intertextual engagement, their shared story makes adaptations centrally identifiable as adaptations.

It is this definition by Hutcheon that will be used when considering *Precious'* positioning as an adaptation. Her definition facilitates a consideration of the unique relationship between the two texts as she sets clear boundaries for what is or is not an adaptation. Furthermore, in considering the film's extended intertextual engagement with *Push*, one can more clearly identify where these two texts align and deviate from one another, giving insight into the different socio-cultural and socio-historic frames that inform these works. Finally, Hutcheon's identification of how the transposition of the core across different media sees adaptations deal 'with the story in formally different ways' (ibid.) facilitates a consideration of how the adaptation of Sapphire's book to film shapes the telling and ultimately the adaptation of this narrative.

Push and *Precious* are separated by time – *Push* was published in 1996 and *Precious* was released in 2009 – author/auteur, medium and industry. As a result of these differences, how the narrative takes shape and unfolds varies. Nonetheless, Daniels makes a clear effort to align *Precious* to *Push* through the naming of the film, *Precious: Based on the Novel Push By Sapphire*; his repeated statements in the DVD extras that he sought to be truthful to the novel; and the film's use of story, first-person narration and dialogue found in the book. In other words, Daniels situates his work as an adaptation by allowing the book to 'haunt' the film through this extended intertextual engagement – reflecting the way that adaptations are 'inherently "palimpsestuous" works' (Hutcheon 2006: 6). Despite this effort to link book and film, the film does at times deviate from the book, as one might expect an adaptation to do. After all, as Hutcheon tells us, adaptation is repetition with variation. To identify and unpack these moments of variation, it is of course important to consider what is repeated and, more specifically, what is at the core of both works. When stripping these two texts back to their core, these works tell a story about an abused poor African-American girl, who strives to overcome her abusive home life, poverty and illiteracy through the navigation of the institutions of the home, education and the state, in order to find her voice and tell her story.

This chapter centrally investigates where and how the two texts intersect and diverge in the telling of this core story. It begins by outlining how both texts address issues of violence and abuse. It then considers the social politics that inform both works as they examine social institutions such as the state, the educational system and the home, before outlining how the texts depict the African-American community, paying particular attention to the figure of the child and the African-American man. The chapter highlights how, despite their shared core, the two texts largely diverge in their ideological framings. It also provides a foundation to make sense of the film independently of the book in the remaining three chapters and introduces some of the broader topics, ideologies and discourses that will be examined throughout the book.

Adapting violence: sexual, emotional, physical and social

Violence and trauma are centripetal forces in Sapphire's book, as Precious recounts moments of abuse continuously and as her story is at all times tethered to her history of abuse. As Caruth states, for trauma victims 'the experience of trauma repeats itself, exactly and unremittingly, through the unknowing acts of the survivor and against his [sic] very will' (1996: 2). Precious is positioned as a trauma victim by the book and establishes herself as one to the reader as she is repeatedly drawn into and gives accounts of her vivid memories of abuse. This trauma haunts the film's narration of the story. However, the loop-like experience of her sexual trauma is diminished as this abuse is only revisited in flashbacks twice. The film consequently spends less time outlining how Precious' trauma invades and dictates all aspects of her life, her relationships and her worldview. It is only in moments of anxiety and worry that the trauma of her past emerges in explicit detail.

In some ways, this limited engagement with the loop-like nature of trauma reflects Daniels' claims in the DVD extras that he wanted the film to be 'lighter'. This lightening of the book's heavy content is further apparent in the way the film tries to escape the trauma and violence of Precious' memories. For example, although flashbacks of her rape are shown from her perspective, these flashbacks never last long. They are interrupted by her imagination as she pictures herself to be, for example, a film star. In her flights of fancy, she is a sexual being who attracts the attention of a handsome light-skinned African-American youth and adoring fans. These imaginings interrupt the abuse and distress Precious experiences. They provide an escape for both the character and the viewer.

The book similarly refers to Precious' use of imagination to escape moments of sexual abuse. Precious remarks on her ability to watch movies on the otherwise blank wall during rapes, or to imagine herself as a dancer. During one recount of being raped, she states:

Then I change station, change *bodies*, I be dancing n videos! In movies!
I be breaking, *fly*, jus' a dancing! Umm hmm heating up the stage at the
Apollo for Doug E. Fresh or Al B. Shure. They love me! Say I'm one
of the best dancers ain' no doubt of or about that!

(Sapphire 1996: 24)

In narrating these moments of escape, the book, like the film, seemingly
provides the reader with a similar avenue to evade her trauma. However, the
book never describes these moments in great detail, and importantly they
are always interrupted by her rape and by her bodily reaction to this rape.
As a result, the reader, like Precious, is denied a complete diversion from
this sexual violence. Thus, rather than facilitating an escape for the reader,
Precious' imaginings alternatively highlight her struggle to cope with a
traumatic experience.

In contrast, as films more commonly align to the showing rather than the
telling mode, it is perhaps not surprising that Daniels' film depicts these
moments of escape in living colour. Where the book tells us that she imagines herself dancing during her rapes, in the film her imagination is corporealised as the audience is transported into her imaginative world. In this way,
the dual image of Precious' rape and imaginings in the book are replaced
and separated in the film, as the change in location, and change in her performance and behaviour disconnect the audience from the rape occurring in
the preceding scene. These daydreams, although interrupted by her mother
throwing water on her or her teacher speaking to her, are not interrupted by
her rape. As such, they offer an escape for both Precious and the audience
that the book does not afford.

Daniels' film also stays away from depictions of abuse that the book
details at greater length. For example, in the book both Carl's and Mary's
sexual abuse of Precious is explained in graphic detail. Precious recounts
Carl's sexual abuse numerous times with assertions such as 'Daddy put his
pee-pee smelling thing in my mouth, my pussy, but he never hold me' (Sapphire 1996: 24–5), or

he squeeze my nipple, bite down on it. I come some more. "*see*, you
LIKE it! You jus' like your mama – you die for it!" He pull his dick out,
the white cum stuff pour out my hole wet up the sheets.

(18)

Precious gives tactile accounts of her experiences of rape as she explains the
feelings, smells and noises tied to these moments of abuse.

In the film, we witness Carl's sexual assault on two occasions. The audience first witnesses Carl from Precious' perspective as he rapes her. The

room is dark, we see his sweaty body as he removes his belt and applies Vaseline before he begins to rape her. Shown in slow motion, the environment in which this rape occurs is made clear as the audience hears him talk to her sexually during the rape, as the springs in the mattress are shown and their creaks heard, as a cat is shown mewing nearby and as Mary watches from the doorway. Like the descriptions provided in the book, the attention given to Precious' environment in this scene, turns her abuse into a clear tactile and corporeal experience for the audience. On the second occasion, the camera looks up into Carl's face from below, aligning the audience with Precious' perspective (see Figure 1.1). This alignment is furthered as he says to her 'Oh you better than your mother'. In using the pronoun 'you' rather than her name, the audience is seemingly addressed by Carl. While the nature of Carl's rape is further corporealised as it includes the audience within this experience, what the film does not depict is Precious' physical and corporeal experience of rape. By adopting Precious' perspective, the audience does not witness in detail how Carl manipulates, controls and handles her body nor how she responds to this treatment. Indeed, Precious and her personalised experience are hidden from the audience, who is instead left to interpret these moments as they look out rather than in. In this way, the book and film both flesh out the main character's experience, but where the film immerses the audience in these moments of rape and creates a tactile understanding of the environment in which they occur, the book both reveals Precious' bodily experiences and feelings while immersing the reader through the *descriptions* of her corporeal experience.

Figure 1.1 The focalisation on Carl from Precious' perspective

Like her account of her father's sexual abuse in the novel, Precious recounts Mary's molestation of her, stating:

> I feel Mama's hand between my legs, moving up my thigh. Her hand stop, she getting ready to pinch me if I move. I just lay still still, keep my eyes close. I can tell Mama's other hand between her legs now 'cause the smell fill the room. Mama can't fit into bathtub no more. Go sleep, go sleep, go to *sleep*, I tell myself. Mama's hand creepy spider, up my legs, in my pussy.
>
> (Sapphire 1996: 21)

The main character's description invites the reader's immersion into this moment of violence as she draws attention to other senses, such as smell. While the reader cannot see this moment, the description provided gives a corporeal understanding of Precious' experience of sexual violence as they come to understand how Mary's touching feels, how Precious is touched, where she is touched and how Mary touches herself. In the film, when her mother sexually assaults her, we see Mary masturbating before we hear her call Precious to the bedroom. The camera cuts away and we do not see the protagonist until the next day. Precious then says that she wishes that Mary would 'stop this shit' and comments about crying after her mother called her to the bedroom. These remarks all point towards the sexual assault that the audience does not actually see or hear. The horror of Mary's act is hidden from the audience and left to their imagination. Where in the book, the detailed account of both Carl's and Mary's assaults cast them as repulsive and reaffirm their similar footing as villains, in hiding Mary's sexual assault, and by repeatedly depicting her verbal and physical attacks on Precious, the film positions the mother as both more violent and as having committed the more taboo action than the father.

This inability to name Mary's crime is reaffirmed in the film's final scene. When Precious' social worker asks Mary to account for the sexual abuse that took place in the home, Mary describes Carl's sexual assault of Precious. However, her sexual abuse of her daughter is only gestured to, in rather vague terms. She says:

> So those things she told you I did to her, who else was going to love me, hm since you got your degree and you know every fucking thing, who was gonna love me, who was gonna make me feel good, who was going to touch me and make me feel good and she made him go away.

Here Mary does not qualify what 'those things' she did to her daughter were. As we have seen Mary verbally and physically assault Precious, it is likely that she is referring to her verbal and physical assault of Precious rather than her sexual assault of her. The potential sexual nature of her reference to 'those things' she did to Precious seems to be more clearly implied when she asks who was going to touch her and make her feel good, suggesting that she made Precious do 'these things' since she held her responsible for making Carl go away. On the other hand, these comments could be read as Mary saying that she could not get another man to 'love' and 'make love' to her. As such, these assertions could be a justification of why she allowed Carl to stay and abuse Precious. The ambiguity around these statements casts a shadow around Mary's sexual assault of her daughter and further reaffirms these actions as taboo.

The film only makes one direct reference to Mary's sexual abuse of Precious. Shortly after she has left Mary's household and while she is staying with Ms. Rain, Precious remarks 'Mama says homos is bad people. But Mama, homos not ones that rape me and what does that make you?' Although initially it might appear that Precious is reflecting on Carl's rape of her, the question 'What does that make you?' suggests that it was Mary's rape of her that she was referring to. Here the film confirms what is implied elsewhere. However, the corporeal nature of this assault is still kept from the audience.

Mary's sexual acts are not the only occurrences that are seemingly too taboo for the big screen. As Meek (2017) points out, Precious' own sexual pleasure during moments of violence is largely erased from the film. The book repeatedly explores how feelings of pain, shame, trauma, sexual pleasure and sexual desire are intertwined in Precious' experience of sexual abuse. She describes her orgasms while being raped as well as the sexual desire she at times feels when thinking of her father. She explains how these feelings are connected with self-hate, shame and repulsion, and her confused feelings become central to how she makes sense of her abuse and her role within that abuse. The film, however, largely ignores this narrative. The only time Precious' complicated experience of rape is indicated is at the end of the film when she states in an internal monologue, 'It was hard tell'n them strangers that what my father did [pause] sometimes felt good'. Here Precious reveals her complicated feelings. However, the film does not seek to unpack or explore these feelings further. Additionally, because there is a long pause before Precious completes the sentence and because she often mumbles and speaks in incomplete sentences, the film opens the space for her statement to be interpreted as her mixed feelings about attending a support group. The pause specifically allows the sentence to be read as an assertion that telling the strangers about her father's abuse was hard, but that talking about the abuse sometimes felt good. Like Mary's devious behaviour, the film masks the book's controversial discussion of the interplay of rape, pleasure, desire and shame.

In addition to adapting the book's narrativisation of sexual violence, Daniels adapts the book's representation of generational violence. For example, while in the book Precious' daughter Mongo is taken into a care home when the state determines that Precious' grandmother is not providing the child with the required care needed to facilitate her development, in the film Mongo seems to be cared for to some degree by Precious' grandmother and is eventually reunited with Precious. In this way, the film creates a more uplifting ending. However, in making this change, the film interrupts the generations of familial dysfunction and violence that shape both Precious' and Mary's life. In the book, the mistreatment of Mongo (who is described as being 'in bad shape' (Sapphire 1996: 84) when she is taken by the state from Precious' grandmother's home), suggests that Precious' grandmother is an abusive figure and that Mary's dysfunction is potentially a product of growing up in an abusive home herself. The circularity of abuse that is implied through the perpetuation of violence from generation to generation consequently points backwards towards an even longer history of abuse, one that ultimately stems from slavery.

In the film, Mary tells her mother that she 'didn't do no better' than Mary. Yet, as Mongo seems relatively cared for and as the film shows early photos of a happy, healthy and well cared for Mary, it undermines the idea that Precious' grandmother was abusive. The film alternatively roots Mary's dysfunction in her relationship with Carl. This is not to suggest that Precious' grandmother is depicted as a 'good' character, she is after all helping Mary to cheat the welfare system in both the book and the movie, and she does nothing in either the book or movie to help Precious escape Mary's and Carl's abuse. However, it is not clear in the film whether her inaction is due to her indifference, misguided beliefs or her fear of Mary, as very little screen time is given to the character, and the other characters spend very little time discussing her role in her granddaughter's life.

In addition to undermining the generational violence the book details, the film masks how violence takes shape within other communities. This occurs as the film singularly focuses on the abuse and violence that is central to Precious' personal history. In contrast, although the book is centrally concerned with telling Precious' story, at the end of the novel, each one of the girls from the Each One Teach One class gives an account of their lives and various (ethnic) backgrounds. These girls' stories are stories of abuse, rape, disease and neglect. Furthermore, as the book gives an account of the support groups Precious attends for incest survivors and for HIV-positive people, the reader is told that 'all kinda girls' are present at the meetings (129), and Precious is surprised to see the young, the old, those of different colour and those from different socioeconomic backgrounds have experienced similar abuse (130). The book consequently extends the troubles she faces beyond a poor African-American community and reframes these as social issues for women more broadly.

In contrast, the film does not give an account of her classmates' lives. Similarly, Precious does not discuss or describe the members in her incest survivor support group, and the film never depicts the group. As such, Precious comes to stand as the central representation of an abused person. As she is African American, her plight and her abuse are presented by the film as an African-American story, rather than one felt more broadly within a community of women. As I will discuss in Chapter 4, this depiction has led to criticisms of the film for the way that it labels the African-American community as dysfunctional. This is not to suggest that the book has not faced similar criticisms. As David (2016: 176) notes, the book risks reaffirming stereotypes of the welfare queen, of Black women-headed households and Black families as dysfunctional. However, in removing the additional scenes and storylines found in the book, the film further narrows and restricts this story of abuse to an African-American community, and reaffirms and perpetuates those stereotypes.

So far, this section has outlined how the film and the book address narratives of physical, sexual and emotional abuse. However, violence also takes shape within the film and the book in the form of a socio-cultural violence. This can be seen through the book's and film's exploration of beauty. Precious' daydreams in the film replace much of her first-person narration where she repeatedly expresses her wish for people to look past her dark skin and large size, to see her as beautiful. Her perception of beauty is rooted in Eurocentric understandings of beauty and in skin-colour prejudice. In the book, she states her belief that lighter-skinned people are more beautiful, intelligent, and worthy of love and care. Her statements demonstrate how her absorption of cultural prejudices have led to her own self-hate and a belief that she needs to be physically different to be loved. The film explores this desire for love as well as her adoption of skin-colour prejudice through her fantasies, as a light-skinned man looks on her with desire. The film's use of a light-skinned man as well as its later depiction of Precious looking in the mirror and imagining herself as a White, thin teen, serves to represent the skin-colour prejudice and misguided perceptions that are explored in the book's dialogue.

Despite the fact that Precious' early prejudices are visually depicted, they are given less space in the film. Their complexity, how they inform her relationships, how they shape both her sense of self and her understanding of who is or is not a victim of abuse are not fleshed out with the same level of intensity in the film. This is perhaps unsurprising, as many of the protagonist's reflections on skin colour are explored through the telling mode in the book. While the film does at times make use of the telling mode through the use of voice-over, as film more consistently makes use of the showing mode, an exploration of Precious' internal struggles becomes more difficult to communicate without the addition of a significantly larger number of scenes and dialogue.

Although the film's more limited engagement with Precious' struggle to overcome her skin tone prejudice may reflect the difficulty of adapting first-person narration within a film without the heavy-handed use of voice-over, the film also reaffirms some of the skin-colour prejudices that the book challenges. As Rountree notes, 'in the film her personal growth is supported by light- and White-skinned individuals, and that reinforces the not so subtle message that White and light-skinned people are morally superior and more compassionate than darker-skinned individuals' (2013: 173; see also Griffin 2014). Though Precious says at the end of the film that despite her initial desire to conform to Eurocentric perceptions of beauty, she is starting to love herself as a dark-skinned and large woman, a message that is reaffirmed when Precious looks in the mirror and sees herself rather than a White teen, the casting choices throughout the film leave the audience with the visual impression of light-skinned African Americans as good and dark-skinned African Americans as welfare cheats and rapists.

Griffin (2014) suggests that the skin-colour bias found in the film is further reinforced to the audience through Precious' imaginings. She asserts:

> why does imagining herself as a White woman offer Precious reprieve from the abusive horrors of her everyday life? From a Black feminist standpoint, it is the imaginative quest for White beauty depicted that strengthens the dominant gaze. . . . *Precious* can be understood as both a vehicle and agent of Whiteness in that the audience is transported into her escapist fantasy realm to bask with her in the glory of White femininity.
>
> (Griffin 2014: 186)

What Griffin highlights is how the film's use of escapism and its privileging of White beauty norms seek to elevate whiteness at the expense of Black beauty and Black subjecthood. I would suggest that this elevation of whiteness through Precious' imagination and through the film's casting choices is a type of violence, as it further entrenches stereotypes of the Black community and it reinforces racial hierarchies.

Critiquing social care

The film and the book offer a critique of the American social system. However, the force behind this critique takes different shapes. As a Black feminist, Sapphire's politics becomes central to her book. In her account of writing the book, she says that in early drafts Precious barely featured in it. She states, 'the first draft of the novel really died under my heavy handed politics about the racism and classism, you know and everything' (quoted in Knopfdoubleday 2009). She then explains that as Precious became more prominent in the book, 'all the politics and all the issues came alive through her' (ibid.). In Sapphire's account, Precious becomes a conduit to express the author's political views.

Notwithstanding the fact that the main character faces abuse at home, the book goes to lengths to highlight the various social systems that fail to support her. For example, after she escapes Mary's home with her newborn, Abdul, Precious returns to the hospital looking for help. After waiting for the nurse that delivered both her babies she states:

> Nurse Butter come. I tell her what happen. I tell her about school, 'bout Farrakhan 'n allah, 'bout maff – how Mr Wicher had told Mrs Lichtenstein I got maff aptitude, and ABCs. How Miz Rain say I'm moving faster through the vowel 'n consonant sounds than even Rita Romero, who is light skinned. I tell her I not hardly seed Little Mongo since my grandmother tooked her and how Abdul my daddy's baby too. . . . Help nurse, help me Miz Lenore. Help me.
>
> (Sapphire 1996: 75–6)

Precious asks for help and tries to lay claim to her entitlement to this help based on her value as a person. She disputes the perception that she is dumb and reaffirms her ability and value against those of lighter colour, highlighting that despite her dark skin she has potential and abilities. She seeks to resolve herself of blame or the label of a jezebel by instead positioning herself as a victim of rape. Yet, rather than assisting Precious, the nurse turns her away and informs Precious that she is 'going off duty' (Sapphire 1996: 76). Left in the hands of the next nurse who is on duty, Precious states that this nurse treats her like she is 'a problem got to be got out they face' (77). This lack of sympathy for the plight of this young mother is extended to all mothers in similar positions as Precious recounts, 'Nurse say lots of people get out hospital wif no place to go, calm down, you not so special' (ibid.). The nurse's response frames this mistreatment and neglects as common and as something that people should accept because it occurs so often. Precious is directed to a homeless centre, instead. At this centre she is afraid, her blanket for the night is stolen, leaving her cold and struggling to keep her newborn warm, and when she wakes in the morning she discovers that her belongings have been stolen. The conditions of the homeless shelter are described as worse than Mary's home, revealing the welfare offered by the state as just as violent and unstable as the dysfunctional home Precious has come from. At this moment, the book confronts the reader with the failure of the social system to help people, and in particular young mothers, in moments of crisis. As Kokkola notes, this scene reveals how 'limited Precious's resources are' (2013: 397). It also reveals the violence and degradation at the heart of the 'help' the social system provides.

In contrast to the book, the film cuts these scenes. Instead, Precious takes refuge in the Each One Teach One school, from which she is then placed comfortably in a halfway house. The removal of the hospital and homeless shelter scenes masks the failing of the social system that Sapphire's book tries to draw the reader's attention to. Instead, the film places more hope in the individuals found within the social system. For example, the film, extending the role of a minor character (an EMS paramedic) in the book, creates nurse John (Lenny Kravitz) who befriends and cares for Precious. The hospital and its staff are consequently depicted as singularly caring and supportive. This is not to suggest that Sapphire's book does not show kindness within the hospital system. When Precious has her first child, she recounts the care and support she received from an EMS paramedic and a nurse. However, the kindness she is shown as a child, though fleeting, completely disappears when she returns to the same hospital at age 16.

Similarly, while Sapphire offers a highly critical review of the welfare system, the film tempers this criticism. It accomplishes this by giving Mrs. Weiss (Mariah Carey), the counsellor provided to Precious by the welfare office, redeemable qualities. In the book, Mrs. Weiss is presented as an adversary for the heroine, as she seems to limit Precious' future by curtailing her education and by getting her involved in a work scheme that will keep Precious in poverty and dependent on the state. In the words of Jarman, Precious learns that 'the social worker and the welfare system function as agents in her oppression' (2012: 175). On the other hand, in the film, while Mrs. Weiss similarly tries to get Precious involved in the same work scheme detailed in the book, the counsellor also serves as a source of emotional support for Precious as she listens to her stories of abuse and as she aligns herself with Precious through her rejection of her mother. For example, in the film's final scene, Mrs. Weiss accuses Mary of allowing Carl to abuse Precious, becomes emotionally upset by Mary's account of Precious' abuse, and when Mary asks Mrs. Weiss to reunite the two after Precious has left, she physically rejects Mary, as she pulls herself away and leaves. Furthermore, the audience is further invited to like Mrs. Weiss and view her as Precious' ally when the latter admits that she likes her.

In contrast, within the book, although Precious describes Mrs. Weiss's shock at Mary's account, the counsellor does not seek to accuse Mary of wrongdoing, nor does she say anything that would suggest that she rejects

Mary for the abuse she has inflicted on Precious. Instead, she tries to encourage Precious to engage with Mary, by asking her to share her writing with her mother, an offer that Precious refuses. Indeed, Precious is highly distrustful of Mrs. Weiss as she expresses confusion about why the counsellor wants her to meet with Mary, and complains that Mrs. Weiss is not trying to help her but is trying to make her dependent on the system by getting her enrolled in the workfare programme. This becomes evident when Precious says 'All this, "What you wanna be?" And "You can talk to me." They ain' no mutherfucking therapist on your side they just flunkies for the "fare"' (Sapphire 1996: 122). Precious cannot trust Mrs. Weiss because she discovers that the therapy sessions she offers are really being used to assess whether Precious is work-ready.

The broader problems with both the scheme the counsellor wishes to enrol Precious on and her role within the social system are explored by the girls in Precious' class and by Ms. Rain (Precious' teacher from Each One Teach One; played by Paula Patton in the film). Precious recounts:

> Jermaine bust in. 'If all they wanna do is place us in slave labor shits and we want to keep going to school, then that means they have a different agenda from us. I wanna work, but not for no mutherfucking welfare check in Central Park. And I be displacing brothers and sisters who really got jobs cleaning up 'cause I'm there working for free. And what kinda shit is it for someone like Precious to have to quit school before she get her G.E.D. to work at some live-in job for old crackers and shit. She'll never make a rise she get stuck in some shit like that!'
> (Sapphire 1996: 122–3)

Through Jermaine's complaint, the book highlights how the work scheme replicates a form of slave labour, how it diminishes the work of people already doing these jobs within the community and how it denies Precious of future uplift. The book consequently reveals the welfare system as one that creates continued dependency. As Jarman asserts in her consideration of the book:

> Although many of these young women rely upon welfare and other social-service programs for survival, they also realise that they must somehow liberate themselves from the oppressive grip of a system designed to exploit them as cheap labor by sacrificing their dreams and human potential.
> (2012: 183)

The book further questions the help Mrs. Weiss can provide when Ms. Rain remarks, 'But what I'm worried about right now is, if this Ms. Weiss is someone they have you talking to to try to work out your history with and you can't trust her, you're not going to get the help you need' (Sapphire 1996: 123). Ms. Rain's doubts highlight the counsellor's inability to help Precious and reflect on how a system that uses personal information to judge what services one is or is not entitled to can only feed mistrust.

The book's critique of individual workers within the social system highlights broader social problems with how social services are run and managed, while the film's depiction of what Daniels describes as 'angels' within the social system draws attention to the care and support that can be given through individual action. The film's celebration of this individual action deemphasises the systemic racism and classism that render the social system ineffective in its support of those in need. It reflects a neoliberal framework that places blame as well as responsibility on individuals rather than on social systems. These differences, while perhaps reflecting the author's and director's diverging political perspectives, also signal their different historical influences, with Sapphire's work informed by the welfare reforms of the 1990s (Michlin 2006: 35) and Daniels' work taking shape during a period in which neoliberalism had become a dominant ideological force in America.

The film's generous depiction of individuals working within the care system, whether that be education, medical services or social welfare, does not suggest that the critiques offered by the book are completely removed by the film. One scene that highlights the limitations of the social system occurs when Precious finds herself homeless after leaving Mary's home and a montage sequence shows Ms. Rain trying to find Precious a place to live. She is shown calling every contact she has, slamming down the phone and picking it up again until at last she finds a place for the young protagonist. These sequences highlight the difficulty of receiving care and support when it is needed. Similarly, when Precious remarks that she plans to rely on the welfare system to help her and Abdul, Ms. Rain warns her against this, telling her to question how much the welfare system has really helped her mother. As she makes these remarks, the camera cuts to an image of Mary living in squalor on her own (see Figure 1.2) Mary's poor living conditions, her unhappy expression and her poorly cared for body, juxtaposed with Ms. Rain's remarks, cast doubt over how much support the welfare system can offer to Precious and people like her.

Interestingly, although the film reaffirms the dangers of relying on the welfare system and paints it as a system of entrapped dependency, it seems to suggest that it is the individual's responsibility not to become reliant on welfare rather than a problem with the system itself. This is evident through Ms. Rains' warnings, which frame the use of welfare as a choice, and through Precious' and her mother's final scene with Mrs. Weiss. Mary says to the counsellor that she does not need any more money, and Precious

Figure 1.2 Visualisation of how welfare has helped Mary

announces to Mrs. Weiss that the whole situation is too much for the welfare counsellor to handle. As she leaves the welfare office with her two children, she seemingly rejects the help she initially sought from the welfare office. However, while the characters seem to choose not to be on welfare, there is no suggestion of how they will survive and manage without welfare help. In presenting welfare as a choice, the film ignores the fact that many people have no choice but to be on welfare, whether this is because they are unable to obtain work or whether this is because they are the working poor. As a result, the film engages with neoliberal ideas of self-choice and self-discipline that put the responsibility on the individual rather than on the state or wider social systems.

Depicting the child and reimagining the African-American man

The book and the film both reinforce and challenge a variety of stereotypical framings of the African-American community. In this section, I specifically explore how the book, through its consideration of the child, problematises stereotypes around who is defined as a child, and how the film, through its depiction of African-American men, challenges some, though not all, negative stereotypes of African-American masculinity. As Chapter 3 gives a detailed account of how the film's depiction of the child shapes and informs the growth and maturation Precious is afforded in the narrative, within this section I wish to consider how the representation of Precious as a child takes shape in the book. This provides the groundwork and counterpoint to later unpack the importance of age in the telling of Precious' coming-of-age story within the film.

Significantly more time is spent reflecting on Precious' childhood in the book. The reader is repeatedly reminded that Precious had her first child at the age of 12. In contrast, the film never states how old Precious was when she had Mongo nor does it reveal how old Mongo is during the course of the film. Instead, Precious' age at the time of Mongo's birth is implied through the casting of Mongo as what appears to be a 3- to 4-year-old child. As Precious is 16 when the audience is introduced to Mongo, the distance between their ages implies that Precious would have been 12 or 13 when Mongo was born. As a result, while the book reaffirms Precious' child status during her first pregnancy, the film leaves it to the audience to assume.

In the book, Precious spends a lot of time reflecting on her experiences as a child – recounting when the abuse began, explaining her emotional decline as a child due to the abuse and outlining her disengagement with the world. She details how other children began to tease her, and she recounts peeing on herself in second grade for fear of getting up from her chair and explains how her teachers gave up on her, asserting 'Finally Principal say, Let it be. Be glad thas all [peeing herself] the trouble she give you. Focus on the ones who *can* learn, Principal say to teacher' (Sapphire 1996: 37). As Jarman notes, these moments in the book are 'blatant examples of the ways social systems designed to protect and sustain Precious fail to even see her' (2012: 174). She is denied her child status as an innocent in need of protection as she is neither protected in the home from sexual and physical abuse nor in the school from bullying, teasing and neglect. The school also fails to intercede in the abuse Precious receives from her parents, which as Jarman points out, is 'written on [and I would add through] her body' (ibid.), with incidences of her wetting herself at school acting as clear signs of her abuse.

As Precious is sexually abused, she is distanced from the childhood purity (read sexual purity) that is commonly associated with the child in the West (discussed further in Chapter 3). The book explores this perception when a nurse asks Precious shortly after she gives birth to Mongo, 'Was you ever, I mean did you ever get to be a chile [child]?' (Sapphire 1996: 13). The nurse's remarks draw the reader's attention to Precious' robbed childhood as well as her distance from childhood purity. However, Precious rejects this statement as she thinks, 'Thas a stupid question, did I ever get to be a chile? I *am* a chile' (ibid.). In rejecting the nurse's remarks, she reclaims and reminds the reader of her entitlement to her child status, and the protection that this status usually affords. As I will demonstrate in Chapter 3, the film does not seek to replicate this claim.

Not only does Precious lay claim to her past identity as a child, she later questions whether others might have done more to protect her at the time. She states:

> I just want to say when I was twelve, TWELVE, somebody hadda help me it not be like it is now. . . . Why no one put Carl in jail after I have baby by him when I am twelve? Is it my fault because I didn't talk to polices?

(Sapphire 1996: 125)

Precious' reflection stakes a claim for the importance of protecting children and for continuing to identify juvenile sexual assault victims as children, as it is this classification that sees them entitled to additional rights and protections (explored further in Chapter 3). Although she questions whether it is her own fault for not speaking to the police, just as her distrust of the welfare system inhibits her from obtaining the emotional support she needs, her inability to trust the police and the wide distrust of the police in her community, similarly prevents her from getting help from this institution. The book, rather than blaming Precious, asks the reader to question what resources are really available to African-American girls and children like Precious. It also asks the reader to question when and why certain children stop being identified as children, and thus not perceived as deserving help and protection.

As Chapter 3 will detail further, the film spends less time outlining the nature of Precious' childhood and does not explore how the limitations of the social system inhibit African-American children from obtaining help. Instead, the film works in the dichotomy of the child (read White Western child) and the nonchild (read the racialised child), and reaffirms racist framings of the Black child in America.

In many ways, the film shies away from the politics that are more forcefully explored in the novel and struggles to challenge some of the regressive stereotypes that surround the African-American community. Nonetheless, as Daniels suggests ('DP/30 . . .' 2013), and as *Precious* seemingly reflects, the film, to some degree, redeems the African-American man. Writing from a Black feminist perspective, Rountree argued that 'Sapphire's *Push* . . . overtly connects with and joins the African American women's literary tradition' (2013: 163). It is thus unsurprising that the care and support Precious finds and which enables her to succeed is rooted strongly within a community of women and within the African-American women writers who Precious identifies as giving her strength. There are male characters that feature in the book in positive roles (Mr. Wicher, who says that Precious has an aptitude for Math, and the EMS paramedic who helps Precious to deliver Mongo). However, their roles are fleeting, and they are not part of the female community that helps Precious to overcome the difficulties in her life. Notably, neither of these characters is African American. Mr. Wicher is described as White and the paramedic as Spanish. The book offers no positive depictions of African-American masculinity.

According to Sapphire, in an earlier version of Geoffrey Fletcher's screenplay, he wanted to readjust this representation of Black men by including what Sapphire describes as 'Steven Spielberg/*Color Purple*-type-father-redemption-reconciliation scenes' (McNeil et al. 2014: 353). Sapphire asked for the removal of these scenes. She asserted that 'the screenwriter was so upset at what he felt would be a blanket condemnation of black men, he asked to have his name removed from the film' (quoted in ibid.). While the film did not seek to redeem Precious' father, in contrast to the book, the film adapts the role of the EMS paramedic, casting Lenny Kravitz, a mixed-race singer and actor, as a nurse that supports and helps Precious along her way. In an interview, Daniels notes that this character was a positive representation of an African-American man within the film ('DP/30 . . .' 2013), and Kravitz's character does reflect this claim as he is incorporated into Precious' broader support system. However, despite the fact that Kravitz has African-American heritage, as a mixed-race American, he also has light skin. As Daniels casts a dark skin man in the role of Carl, the director's depiction of African-American manhood reaffirms a skin tone bias that positions light-skinned African-American men as good and dark-skinned African-American men as criminals, rapists and deviants.

Although Daniels includes a redemptive male figure within the film, this is not to suggest that he abandons all the feminist politics that the book communicates through its depiction of Precious' female-centred community and support system. As Griffin notes:

> Ms. Rain, alongside her light-skinned partner Katherine, also signifies Black feminism which is visually confirmed by the "for colored girls who considered suicide when the rainbow is enuf" (Shange 1975) print on display in their home. Additionally, Ms. Rain embodies Black feminism by taking Precious in and fiercely advocating to get her into a halfway house.
>
> (2014: 188)

Thus, though Daniels' film moves away from the exclusively feminine space Sapphire creates, he does not eradicate all the Black feminist ideals at the heart of her book.

Conclusion

When comparing the storytelling modes of these two works, it becomes clear that although each work narrates how a young girl overcomes the adversities in her life to find her voice, the politics surrounding this consideration varies and is at times at odds with one another. Sapphire's strong Black feminist politics finds voice through the characters, but the film significantly softens this voice and at times reinforces stereotypes around race and skin tone that are challenged by the novel. Even though both works seek to highlight the shortcomings of the social system, Sapphire's book draws attention to the systemic issues that prevent Precious from getting the help she needs, while Daniels' film provides a neoliberal reading of the system that promotes individual action rather than systemic change. As the remaining chapters will demonstrate, this difference in part reflects the politics of colour-blind racism and neoliberalism that were dominant when the film was produced. This type of politics was the product of shifts in the national discourse around race during the Obama presidency.

Having created a platform to begin to identify how the film builds on and moves away from the novel, the remainder of this book unpacks how the film takes shape in its own right. It considers the role genre plays in the adaptation of the story, how the film (re)imagines narratives of Black girlhood, and whether the critical reception of the film gives insights into the politics that were dominant at the time of its release.

2 *Precious* and the conventions of youth films

This chapter considers how *Precious* engages with and deviates from the broader conventions of youth films. More specifically, it examines how the film's relationship with the youth cinema genre gives insight into the construction of African-American girlhood. In many ways, making sense of and defining youth films as a genre is not without its difficulties. This is because while scholars would agree that the genre exists, how to define the parameters of the genre has proven difficult. Scholars such as Tropiano (2006: 11) and Doherty (2002: 2) define youth cinema as films made about teens, for teens. Driscoll (2011: 1) similarly defines the genre as centrally about youths. However, she varies slightly by suggesting that these films target an adolescent rather than a teen audience (2–3). Driscoll separates the teen audience from the adolescent one as she sees the concept of teen as too narrow (ibid). While she is not entirely explicit in her definition of adolescence, she more loosely associates the term with socio-cultural understandings of youth rather than the empirical labelling of teens as bound by a specific age range (ibid). Regardless, while Driscoll moves a consideration of intended audience beyond the narrow confines of the teen, like Tropiano and Doherty, she still highlights the importance of an intended youthful audience in the classification of youth cinema. Finally, although scholars such as Shary (2014: 13) and Nelson (2019: 10) more centrally identify youth films as films that feature young people in leading roles, both nonetheless make reference to an intended youth audience (Shary 2014: 3, Nelson 2019: 10), even if this is in a limited way, with Nelson also emphasising the importance of these films' thematic attributes when defining the genre (ibid).

In contrast, Benton et al. (1997: 83), Lewis (2014: 2), Smith (2017: 8–10) and Colling (2017: 2), all question whether intended audiences should be seen as a criterion for the genre. As Benton et al note:

> film researchers should keep in mind that people of all ages attended and still attend teen films. Popular films about adolescents are also

DOI: 10.4324/9781315545547-3

expressions of larger cultural currents. Studying the films is important for understanding an era's common beliefs about its teenaged population within a broader pattern of general cultural preoccupations.

(1997: 83)

This suggests that the genre is not simply about or for the teen, but about a wider understanding and engagement with what that teen is understood to be within a broader culture and society. From this perspective, there is a risk that if the genre is defined as films for teens, these broader socio-cultural discourses and framings could become obscured. Furthermore, as Lewis points out, as the film industry has sought to 'embrac[e] the adolescent as its ideal audience', the majority of the films produced by the industry have this audience in mind (2014: 2). In other words, if one were to take the targeting of teen audiences as a measure of a teen film, then the genre might become overly inclusive. For these scholars, youth, youth culture, shared thematic content and/or aesthetic considerations serve as central ways for defining the genre.

Scholars generally agree that youth films engage with narratives of coming-of-age, struggles with authority, sexual development and the institutional management of young people. Shary (2005, 2014), Shary and Seibel (2007), Driscoll (2011), Lewis (2014) and to a large extent Nelson (2019) unpack these films and narrative conventions from a socio-cultural perspective. However, these narrative and thematic elements, and the genre as a whole, have also been explored in relation to its production history (see Tropiano 2006, Nelson 2019) as well as its aesthetic appeal (Smith 2017, Colling 2017).

As noted by Driscoll (2011: 4), early scholarship on youth cinema tends to focus on American-made films. Reflecting the lack of diversity in Hollywood youth films, much of the early scholarship on youth cinema focused on White youth culture. This is perhaps not surprising when considering that even in the year *Precious* was released, 2009, the vast majority of Hollywood youth films, like *The Lovely Bones* (Jackson, 2009), *Race to Witch Mountain* (Fickman, 2009), *Whip It* (Barrymore, 2009), *An Education* (Scherfig, 2009), *I Love You Beth Cooper* (Columbus, 2009) and *Fired Up* (Gluck, 2009), featured White Western (often middle class) teens as the leading characters. In many ways, the definition of the genre in relation to White Western frames simply reflects the limited number of films about African-American youths or minority groups produced in Hollywood. As a consequence, it is difficult for scholars to identify patterns and norms from the limited sample of African-American youth films, and in particular African-American youth films about girlhood, available. The dominance of the White Western youth film, its centrality to defining the genre and the limited portrayals of minority groups in youth films are all reasons why this chapter to a large extent unpacks how *Precious* takes shape in relation to the White Western frames associated with the genre.

However, Hollywood is not completely devoid of African-American representation even if it is limited in representations of African-American girlhood. A notable exception is the ghetto youth films of the 1990s. As Shary highlights, while before the 1990s few films sought to depict African-American youths (2014: 148), the ghetto youth films focused on male African-American characters. These films took the strong moralising tone of 'crime doesn't pay' (ibid.) and depicted only those who found their way out of their African-American communities as successful characters (153). Unsurprisingly, 'Critics often attacked the films as beholden to the expectations of routinely white audiences, or as glorifying the image of violent young black men who mistreat women and fail to achieve their ambitions' (148). By the mid-1990s spoofs of these films began to be produced, albeit in a limited capacity. These spoofs drew attention to the stereotypical way male African-American youths were portrayed in Hollywood.

While the vast majority of films about African-American teens produced during this time, particularly in Hollywood, focused on male characters, films like *Just Another Girl on the I.R.T.* (Harris, 1993) and later *Our Song* (McKay, 2000) and *On the Outs* (Silverbush and Skolnik, 2004) cast African-American girls in leading roles. These films, like ghetto youth films, tended to focus on the difficulties associated with living in the inner city. Where crime, drug use and violence tended to feature centrally in films about male African-American youths, teen pregnancy took on a greater role in films about African-American girlhood. Notably, unlike many of the ghetto youth films, none of these African-American girlhood films were produced and/or distributed by the Hollywood studios. Instead, they were produced by independent companies that tried to fill this gap with a small number of productions. In this respect, it is clear that *Precious* aligns strongly with these early films. Not only are the topics of teen pregnancy and the focus on an impoverished, if not dysfunctional, inner-city African-American community central to all these films, Precious was also a film that was produced by independent production companies and released by indie distributor Lionsgate.

Despite Precious' alignment with these early depictions of African-American girlhood, as this chapter demonstrates, *Precious* does not fit neatly within the confines of the youth cinema genre. If one considers the movie in relation to early definitions of the genre as films about teens, made for teens, *Precious* uncomfortably fits in these parameters. As already mentioned and will be discussed further in Chapter 3, the protagonist's teen status is often not apparent. The movie's positioning as a film for teens or even adolescents is also unclear. On the one hand, the film closes with a dedication to all precious girls, a strategy that, while it might not address a broad teen audience, seems to speak to, or at least call to mind, a part of the teen population, namely abused and impoverished African-American girls. The film is rated R, which suggests that while it will not be consumed by American teens under 17 without parental permission, teens 17 years and older still have access to it. In the UK, where the film is rated 15, a larger teen audience can see it. Yet the marketing of and the critical responses to the film seem to position it as one that should be viewed by all people (read adults) rather than teens specifically (as detailed further in Chapter 4). Teen audiences are also not mentioned in any of the promotional materials for *Precious*. As such, while it may be accessible to teens, it is not clear that the film has been created with the teen market specifically in mind.

If one were to move away from these early definitions of the youth film and instead explore the ways that *Precious* aligns with the thematic elements of the genre, as I do shortly, it similarly becomes apparent that the film does not comfortably fit within these thematic frames. One might even reasonably question why it is worth contextualising the film in relation to youth cinema at all when it seems to, at least to some degree, resist the genre as it has largely been defined by scholars. What I want to suggest is that by detailing how *Precious* draws on and at times sets itself against the generic makeup of the youth film, and in particular the school film subgenre, one can unpack how it distances its depiction of African-American girlhood from the White Western frames of youth and youth culture, and constructs expectations and norms for an imagined African-American girlhood. In his contemplation of the 'school film' subgenre, Shary notes, 'in most school films, the educational setting becomes an index for youth issues, featuring a variety of youth culture styles and types' (2014: 11). These films centre around narratives of 'individual growth', 'educational achievement' and 'social acceptance' (30). While *Precious* similarly focuses on these types of narratives, films in this subgenre tend to be upbeat and fun. As *Precious* is a more challenging film, the movie's tone sees it align with what Shary describes as the moralising African-American youth films that seek to contrast the promises of education with the dangers of 'street' life (38). Although *Precious* is not a film about organised crime and gangs, the movie nonetheless roots education as the solution to Precious' various difficulties.

In many ways, *Precious*' employment of youth genre conventions sees the film align with three of the four racist discourses Pimentel and Sawyer identify in the motion pictures, namely that African Americans are represented as 'an academic and social underclass that need to be rescued', that African-American communities are violent and dysfunctional, and that to succeed African Americans must escape their community (2011: 100). On the one hand, this chapter demonstrates how these stereotypical and racist depictions of the African-American community take shape as *Precious* is distanced from White Western youth culture and aligned with stereotypical elements of African-American school and African-American youth film genres. On the other hand, as the film is not a wholly regressive or stereotypical text, the chapter considers how the distancing of *Precious* from White Western youth culture and youth films also at times enables it to explore and question the opportunities and narratives for success and growth made available to impoverished African-American girls on screen.

Youth films: *Precious* and narratives of acceptance, success and popularity

Describing Hollywood youth films Shary asserts that 'the films tend to follow the dreams of success and popularity that many young people share, and youth culture is portrayed as primarily White, middle class, nonreligious, suburban, and fun' (2007: 1). Precious is neither White nor middle class, the movie is set in an urban environment and it largely focuses on difficult subjects. Nonetheless, like many youth films, *Precious* follows its young protagonist's dreams for success, acceptance and popularity. The film plays with this generic convention by contrasting the dreams and ideals found in Precious' fantasies with the outcomes of her educational pursuit. Through this contrast, the film critiques the narratives of success, acceptance and popularity that are available to African-American girls in the media by suggesting that these narratives fail to depict aspirations that are readily available to impoverished African-American girls.

The film gives direct insight into Precious' dreams through depictions of her fantasies. In her imagination, she is often richly dressed. Her clothing, jewellery, hairstyle and makeup suggest that Precious' imagined success is one of wealth. She pictures herself as sexually attractive, as she dreams of a young man lusting after her, and desirable, as crowds of people take photos of her and call out her name. Her imagined self seems to be a celebrity, namely an actor, fashion icon or music video dance star. Precious' desire for success, popularity and acceptance is rooted in her superficial understanding of celebrity popular culture.

However, the acceptance, success and popularity Precious achieves occur in ways that she does not imagine and which celebrity popular culture does not narrate for her. For example, despite Precious' desire to learn to read and write, after attending her first class at Each One Teach One, she says:

> Ms. Rain said we gonna read and write in our notebooks every day. How we supposed to do that? But then she see the worry on my face

and she say, 'The longest journey begin with a single step.' Whatever the fuck that supposed to mean.

Her inability to understand Ms. Rain's advice highlights her struggle to work towards a dream of literacy let alone literacy itself. Her powerlessness to imagine her literacy is evident in her fantasies, as none include depictions of her reading or writing. Although popular culture gives Precious a framework to imagine herself within celebrity culture, she seemingly lacks a frame of reference to imagine what academic success might look like for a person like her.

Similarly, Precious neither fantasises about forming friendships nor vocalises a dream to obtain friends. Instead, the friendships she finds catch her off guard. For instance, when the girls are at a museum, one of them, upset by the others' behaviour, grabs Precious' hand. Precious proclaims, 'Ain't nobody ever grabbed my hand like that before'. At this moment, a close-up shot is shown of Precious' hand being held without her holding back (see Figure 2.1). This shot is immediately followed by a secondary close-up shot of Precious' face where she looks caught off guard and unsure of how to respond to the gesture. Her shock at this human contact and the friendship it implies, as well as her decision not to hold the hand back emphasises her previous, and in some ways ongoing, isolation. It draws attention to her hollow imagining of popularity, as defined by public admiration rather than concrete, bilateral and material relationships. Within the film, the gap between what Precious dreams, and the fulfilment, support and joy she finds through her obtainment of friends, suggests that popular

Figure 2.1 Precious' hand is held by a friend

culture does not provide African-American girls like Precious with the representations they need to imagine their future selves and relationships, nor does it provide them with the stories they need as a reference to find their own path.

The final narrative of acceptance found in the film, which Precious does not actively pursue but ultimately obtains, is self-acceptance. Throughout the film, Precious often dreams that she is someone other than who she is, whether that be a celebrity, a thin, blond, White girl or an Italian character from the movie *La Ciociara* (or *Two Women*; De Sica, 1960). However, at the end of the film Precious demonstrates self-acceptance when she declares:

> Last week, Ms. Rain asked us to write down what we wanna be like. I wrote that I'd be real skinny, with light skin and long hair and she read it and said I'm beautiful like I am. But somehow, right now, and I don't know why, but I think she right.

Precious mistakes Ms. Rain's question, which seems to be asking her to imagine who she might become and what goals she has for the future, rather than who she might be if she could superficially change her appearance. Precious' response shows her internalisation of European beauty norms, and how these values prevent her from imagining herself and her future as she is within the world.

In acknowledging that Ms. Rain might be right that Precious is beautiful, she accepts herself and begins to recognise her material place in the world. This is apparent when she turns to a younger abused African-American girl and gives her an orange scarf. This scarf was given to Precious by a fairy godmother-like figure during the first fantasy the audience witnesses. Precious carries this scarf throughout the film. In giving away the scarf, she lets go of her fantasies and past trauma. She stops wishing to be someone else and accepts who she is. This message is reiterated as she turns and looks in the mirror. No longer looking at an imagined reflection of a White girl, Precious sees herself as a material and fully fledged person in the world, and centrally, as a person that matters. The film uses the contrast between her self-discovery and the self she imagines to reiterate the limited narratives of success and accomplishment that Precious has to draw upon. In this way, the film's engagement with the genre's narratives of success, popularity and acceptance problematises the dreams that are readily available to young impoverished African-American girls and illustrates how these dreams fail to provide them with the frames and avenues that will lead them to the attainment of these things.

As part of Precious' coming-of-age narrative, she must learn the hollowness of her own imaginary and the value of more modest dreams. Yet the abandoning of these dreams is not simply a move away from the artificiality of popular culture, but a movement away from the dominance of White cultural narratives of beauty and success. It is interesting to note that many of Precious' dreams are rooted in White culture. As Griffin notes (drawing on the work of bell hooks), 'During these fantasy scenes, we are introduced to her idealized life, largely characterized by appeals to light/Whiteness and middle- to upper-class status. . . . Hence, Precious' fantasies reveal her imagined escapism as a reconstitution of "white supremacist capitalist patriarchy"' (2014: 185). As these dreams offer Precious no permanent or readily available avenue out of her situation, they are depicted as limiting to the character's development. It is only when she lets go of these fantasies, embraces Black history and recognises herself as a beautiful Black woman, that her transformation is complete. This would seem to create a progressive narrative that facilitates an understanding of African-American beauty, friendship and success. Yet, as becomes apparent in the next section and as I have already gestured towards in Chapter 1, while the film's generic engagement with narratives of success, acceptance and popularity challenges White ideals within youth culture, the film's casting decisions and use of stock characters undermine the strength of this narrative.

Youth films: stock characters and the saviour teacher

Youth films commonly rely on stock characters (Tropiano 2014: x). Although *Precious* does not depict jocks, nerds and popular girls, it does maintain the saviour teacher figure that is often found in African-American school films. As Shary notes, 'movies have presented inspirational teachers alternately as saviors of troubled youth, replacements for ineffective parents, and visionaries who motivate learning and success within diffident teenagers' (2014: 36). Cast in this role, Ms. Rain provides the direction, support and hope Precious needs to escape her home life, obtain her education and find a support network that enables her success. In her consideration of Ms. Rain's role in her life, Precious asserts, 'Some folks have a light around them that shine for other people. . . . That's Ms. Rain to me'. Her teacher 'shines' for her by giving her life hope and direction. She is depicted as creating this hope through three means, by assuming the role as inspirational educator, surrogate mother and social worker.

In all three of these roles, Ms. Rain motivates and enables Precious' learning. As a teacher, she gives the young protagonist a voice and introduces her to a world beyond her family, immediate community and social services. She does this by first giving Precious a journal to write in. As this book is read and responded to by Ms. Rain, Precious' voice is validated as it is given a clear direction and is heard and engaged with. Furthermore, as character voice-overs provided by Precious and her teacher give the audience access to these words, the protagonist's voice consequently finds a wider secondary audience.

Ms. Rain also exposes Precious to important historical figures who shaped the world she currently lives in and who can provide her with the 'light' needed to find a better tomorrow (see Figure 2.2). This is evident after her teacher takes the class to a museum. Precious is shown sitting alone in the classroom, framed at the centre of the shot, as the camera traverses the room and depicts different moments in Black history, American history and world history, including the Tiananmen Square protests, which though historically have yet to occur in the year the film is set, are seemingly intended to display her broader understanding of the world. The scene includes images of time, arts and culture, a flower and the continent of Africa, all projected onto the classroom walls. As Precious proclaims 'I'm going to teach my baby all this', she takes ownership of this learning and demonstrates the importance of this knowledge to her life and the life of her children. The education Ms. Rain provides transforms the young character's understanding of the world and her place in it. It also suggests that education breaks the cycles of abuse within African-American families, as Precious decides to share her success and transformative knowledge with her children, rather than excluding them from this education, as her mother is shown doing.

In addition to her role as an educator, Ms. Rain becomes positioned as a surrogate mother. In this role, she is the self-sacrificing and nurturing figure that is otherwise missing from Precious' life. This is evident in the way that Ms. Rain takes her in when she lacks a home, in her emotional investment in the young girl's life via her motivating responses in the diary, in her visit

Figure 2.2 The film's representation of Precious' transformation through education

to the hospital after Precious has given birth and in her declaration about her love for Precious when the latter is at her lowest ebb. The teacher gives her student the emotional care and support that her mother does not provide and equips the character with the strength needed to continue her studies.

Finally, in her role as saviour, Ms. Rain embodies the idealised social worker, though Precious specifically reminds the audience that she is not a social worker. After the young protagonist runs away from her home with her 3-day-old son, her teacher is depicted trying to find her student a home. Precious states 'I could tell by Ms. Rain's face, I ain't going to be homeless no more . . . I feel bad for her, she just an ABC teacher. She ain't no social worker . . . but she is all I could think of'. Ms. Rain's dogged persistence stands in contrast with the social worker Precious meets with, who fails to remove her from the home she knows to be sexually and physically abusive. Thus, while Ms. Rain is not a social worker, her drive, care and ability to find solutions for her student places her as the idealised figure of the social worker, where the social worker acts as fairy godmother. It is the combination of these three roles that sees Ms. Rain positioned as a saviour.

While Ms. Rain is depicted heroically, the film's adherence to these genre norms sees it reiterate stereotypical depictions of Black youths, in which the only way for them to survive is to distance themselves from their community by assuming middle-class knowledge and understanding through education (see Pimentel and Sawyer 2011). Considering the moralising discourse found in African-American youth films, Reid notes that the films of the 1990s 'express[ed] the belief that young black adults have lost faith in their community's ability to assist them to better their lives' (2000: 25). Like the films from the 1990s, films from the 2000s that depicted African-American youths, such as *Akeelah and the Bee* (Atchison, 2006) and *The Blind Side* (Hancock, 2009), reiterated these beliefs. In privileging middle-class values found in the education system, and particularly in the Each One Teach One classroom, *Precious* mirrors other African-American youth films that stereotypically and regressively suggest that 'African-Americans do not possess skills to succeed on their own and [that they] look to others for provisions' (Pimentel and Sawyer 2011: 101).

Ms. Rain, while African American, is depicted as a middle-class African American. This class standing is apparent through her academic knowledge and through Precious' recognition of both her teacher's class standing and the benefits it carries. When staying in her home Precious proclaims in reference to Ms. Rain and her partner Katherine, 'they talk like tv channels I don't watch. I'm glad Abdul here to listen to them though cause I know they smart. I don't understand a word they saying'. In the background, the two women are depicted speaking in analogies and idioms. This style of speech serves to indicate that they are educated and therefore from a different community than the impoverished community Precious comes from.

In this scene, the women are in a well-decorated and inviting home, which reaffirms their class status and relative wealth, particularly as it stands in contrast with Mary and Precious' home, which is dark, worn and filled with rubbish. Precious recognises the value of being surrounded by and learning from these women, as her monologue emphasises her educational distance from them and the positive impact they will have on Abdul, who would otherwise not be exposed to such people within her own community. The young girl's admiration for these two women positions them, and their educational and class standing, as a resource for her and her children's future success. Her monologue invites the audience to view Ms. Rain, and the class standing she embodies, as better able to provide Precious with help and assistance. On one level, the division between Precious and the community she comes from and Ms. Rain and the community she embodies reflects the estrangement between poor and middle-class African Americans in contemporary America that Speed (2001) identifies in her consideration of Black college films. On another level, the positioning of her teacher as better set to help the young protagonist to grow and develop reflects the stereotype that 'African-Americans can only achieve success by escaping the confines of their African-American communities' (Pimentel and Sawyer 2011: 103), in this case a poor African-American community.

In addition to furthering depictions of these community divisions, the casting of Ms. Rain reaffirms the capital of lightness/whiteness in these divisions. The character and her partner are played by thin and light-skinned actresses, despite the fact that in the book Ms. Rain is described as having dark skin. While both women have African-American heritage, Paula Maxine Patton is of mixed race and both women have features that are prized within European standards of beauty. As Rountree points out, this casting is problematic in so far as 'the white and light skinned characters are portrayed as those persons who possess compassion and a willingness to assist others . . . while the darker skinned characters, Precious's mother and father, are abusers' (2013: 172). She goes on to argue that these casting decisions 'perpetuate the stereotypes that whiteness equates to purity and goodness and blackness equates to lewdness and evil' (ibid.). Ms. Rain is not the only light-skinned or White character to help Precious, but as she is positioned in the saviour role, her purity and goodness are even further exaggerated. While the film questions the value of whiteness found in celebrity and youth cultures, the casting of the middle-class, light-skinned Ms. Rain as the saviour reinforces the idea that White/light-skinned middle-class values and education are the only avenue for hope, escape and renewal for the main character. The film creates the impression that the purity of

White culture embodied through education, and those who align themselves with White middle-class values, provide the path out of the repressive and abusive African-American community embodied by dark-skinned and poor African-American characters.

Reimagining heterosexual romance and the youth film

In addition to the tropes and stock character roles described previously, youth films tend to conform to specific narrative conventions. As Driscoll notes, these films tend to centre around heterosexual romance, conflicts and or relationships with family members, teachers or peers, 'the institutional management of adolescence', graduation and transformation (2011: 25). Furthermore, she argues that these narrative conventions tend to be moralising in nature. Indeed, *Precious* engages with these conventions in a moralising way. The main character's desire to obtain an education and literacy is continuously at the centre of this film. The movie explores how she navigates and resolves conflicts in her home life, how she develops friendships and how she achieves transformation as she gains confidence and understanding through her educational pursuits. However, where heterosexual romance is often explored in the teen film through a character's longing and pursuit of a specific love interest, Precious' desires for heterosexual romance are confined to fantasy. As she notes in the film, she has never had a boyfriend, though she would like one with light skin and a good haircut. This desired romantic partner is depicted in her fantasies, but he is not based on any individual in her community. As her fantasies are often hyperbolic and far removed from her everyday life, the inclusion of heterosexual romance within this space casts it as hyperbolic and unlikely.

Precious' ability to appear as a sexually desirable subject is often questioned in the film. When she is spoken to by boys in a sexualised manner, the boys' dialogue and behaviour suggest that they are harassing and bullying Precious rather than asserting their desire for her. One boy tells her, 'let me get some of that sweet ass, orca'. Despite the sexualised nature of his remark, the use of the word 'orca' reaffirms that he is insulting the protagonist by comparing her size to a whale. His feigned desire for her suggests that her size makes her undesirable. Precious recognises the nature of the boy's remarks as she states in a voice-over 'I wish they'd leave me alone' directly before one boy claims 'she's stupider' and another boy in the group pushes her to the ground as the group laughs.

The film emphasises the disconnect between how boys in her community perceive her with her imagined desirability in her fantasies. For example, immediately following the scene described previously, the camera cuts to Precious' fantasy world, where she is shown dancing in front of a screaming crowd in a sheer, silk and feathered outfit. Her love interest stands at the side of the stage looking on lustfully as she dances. Inviting him on stage with her, the two dance as he begins to lick her ear (see Figures 2.3 and 2.4). At this moment, she is the desired subject she wishes to be, but which she is not perceived as by the boys in her community. This contrast suggests that her dream of being both obese and desired is a fantasy. As Precious never obtains a boyfriend or is desired by a male character beyond her fantasies,

Figure 2.3 Precious' imagined desirability

Figure 2.4 Precious' imagined romance

the film closes down the possibility of reading the obese youth as a desirable subject, and more importantly one that might have a romantic narrative of their own to tell.

The boys who harass Precious are dark-skinned African Americans. They stand in contrast with her imagined love interest who is a light-skinned African American. This imagined love interest, not only desires Precious, but in other fantasies he is depicted staring at her lovingly or standing by her side supportively. In this way, the film continues to highlight the division between light- and dark-skinned African Americans by holding the real and imaginary boys in stark contrast. Writing particularly about this point, Griffin points out, 'the audience can surmise that blackness is cruel and ominous while Whiteness is enjoyable and promising' (2014: 186). The use of the romance narrative within the film consequently provides the platform to perpetuate stereotypes that see the dark body as deviant and threatening, and the obese body as undesirable.

Institutionalisation of adolescence

Despite the dark nature of the film, Precious is not without optimism. This optimism takes shape through her resolve of familiar conflicts, her negotiation of peer and teacher relationships, and her navigation of the institutions of the home, school and welfare system. Precious' successful navigation of these relationships and institutions facilitates her transformation, finding peace and happiness, and taking ownership of her life. The film creates a moralising discourse, in which to obtain success the main character must commit fully to her studies, she must leave behind her family and dysfunctional community, she must obtain friendships and relationships with those who are middle class or who are at least trying to escape their poor backgrounds and she must reject the 'help' provided by the welfare system, taking responsibility for her future through her goals for self-improvement.

As a social issues 'school film', *Precious* focuses on the young protagonist's education and the circumstances that impede her from obtaining this education. Just over 35 minutes of screen time are spent depicting classroom scenes, just over 21 minutes depicting her home life and just over 17 minutes depicting her engagement with social services. Where Driscoll suggests that the teen film is 'centered on the institutional life of adolescents at home and school' (2011: 3), Precious' dysfunctional life and upbringing see her narrative trajectory further entwined in the additional institutional forces of the welfare state. Her poor Black female body is made to navigate the adult institution of the state where she at once is asked to take responsibility for her dependency on the state while submitting to this dependence. The liminality of this position consequently sees her body constrained in ways that

White middle-class and privileged youths found in many Hollywood school films often are not. It is also notable that even when White youths on screen have contact with the welfare system, their involvement with social workers often centres around whether the adolescent should be taken into the care of the state when their parents are dysfunctional. In contrast, though Precious is not yet 18 and thus not a legal adult, her engagement with her social worker focuses on whether the state should financially support her rather than whether they should remove her from the care of an abusive parent.

The welfare state requests two things from Precious in order to take her on as a dependent. The first requirement is that she makes a confession about her dysfunctional home life. When meeting with the social worker, Precious is asked to talk about her relationship with her father. When she is evasive about discussing her home life, she is told that if she wants a cheque, she is going to have to talk to the social worker about her relationships. This confession is a requirement that ensures her submission to the state. In conforming herself to the state's requirements, she surrenders her own wishes, admits her need for dependency and makes herself vulnerable to the state, which in turn judges and assesses how she will be helped based on the 'need' she articulates. The second requirement is that she takes part in a government-run work scheme. As Precious explains the exploitative nature of the work scheme to her Each One Teach One peers and Ms. Rain, it becomes apparent that the second form of submission to the state secures her continued dependence as the work scheme will inhibit her from obtaining her education, from being a mother and from saving enough money to escape from a reliance on the state. In short, part of Precious' coming-of-age is to learn that the welfare state is not a solution, that it will not lead her to the life she hopes to live and that it will require her to repeatedly submit herself to the will of the state as a dependent.

Although the welfare state is at times depicted as repressive and Precious' navigation of it becomes a means to critique aspects of it, Precious' early expectation that the welfare state can enable her to live independently reveals her lack of knowledge and understanding of the roles and limitations of welfare. It also suggests that she has a limited understanding of how she could live beyond poverty. As the film does not depict any characters within her community who are working and succeeding, she seemingly has no role models that demonstrate how she might live without welfare. Precious' changing relationship and understanding of the welfare state becomes a means to rethink how she plans to live and to move beyond the examples set for her in her community.

Similarly, the institution of the family, which is so broken that even the state cannot, and later will not, fix it, is another obstacle that Precious must overcome. However, in this effort she must learn what the family should be, which is framed by the film as one that should be loving, supportive and free of violence. Her home life is marked by a level of abuse less commonly depicted in Hollywood youth films. This is not to suggest that incest is not a common feature in youth films more generally. As Shary notes, incest is commonly found in global youth cinema (Shary 2007: 4). However, it is a less common feature of Hollywood youth films and it is the repeated depictions of physical, verbal and/or sexual abuse and the centrality of that abuse to the narrative that heightens the dark nature of this film. Precious' negotiation of the institution of the family is a negotiation of a failed family. Like young people depicted in many other youth films, she must learn to overcome the limitations and constraints of home by either abandoning her existing family to create a new family within a network of friends or to recover her own family through reconciliation. The film explores both these avenues as Precious develops a family network out of friendships made in the Each One Teach One school. These friends discuss their lives, provide company, reflect on difficulties and encourage each other in their educational pursuits. Despite the fact that the girls are based in New York, notably these friendships are not formed from within Precious' immediate community but take shape within the classroom.

In contrast, Precious' family serves to repress her, as her mother discourages her from obtaining education and as her abusive behaviour isolates her daughter from others. Ultimately, reconciliation with her family proves impossible. The failings of the family as an institution mirror and reflect racist and stereotypical framings of the African-American community. As Pimentel and Sawyer argue, there is the flawed and racist perception that 'African-Americans who possess skills to succeed must rely on others for help in escaping their ill-fated communities and . . . African-American communities obstruct promising African-Americans from achieving success' (2011: 103). Like the community within *Precious*, the family obstructs the main character's success. The film consequently perpetuates myths that frame those within the African-American community, whether they are part of a family or the immediate community, as only ever a source of repression.

At the start of the film, the institution of education is also framed as dysfunctional and as a holding tank. Precious is in a classroom with younger pupils who are misbehaving and unengaged. It is not evident that these students are learning in the classroom, and Precious' own account of her academic ability (having obtained A grades when she cannot read or write) suggests that she has been unable to learn and develop in this environment. The dysfunction of the school is exaggerated as the principal is overheard discussing a student who, having been expelled, is on campus without permission. This representation of the students as out of control and the staff as struggling to obtain order presents a third institution that is seemingly broken when rooted within Precious' immediate community.

After being expelled for her pregnancy, the young protagonist is enrolled in an alternative school in the orderly class of Ms. Rain, who is progressive in her teaching and middle class in her ideological instruction. Some Black history is gestured towards when Precious reflects on what she has learned. However, this is confined to successful Black political figures, namely, Martin Luther King Jr., who came from a middle-class background and Shirley Chisholm, who, while parented by working-class parents, in her early years lived in the West Indies with her grandmother where she received a British education. She later attended public schools in Brooklyn, Brooklyn College and Columbia University where she obtained a master's degree (Michals 2015). In short, these African-American figures are tied to middle-class culture and middle-class values. Furthermore, as the students' trip to the museum suggests, they are also taught about conventional subjects, which reflect an educational system that has long privileged White male history and perspectives. In this environment Precious begins to learn, once again highlighting the value of middle-class culture.

Precious' immersion in and embrace of this institution create the hopeful undertone that is commonly associated with films within the social issues school film subgenre. This institution is also accredited with Precious' escape from her broken home, as the support system she develops at the school enables her to leave Mary's household and the repressive grip of the welfare state. We see the potential this institution offers clearly near the end of the film when Precious discusses her plans to graduate from 8th grade, obtain a high-school degree and go to college. The film consequently frames education as the means of escape from abuse and poverty. Precious' newfound confidence suggests that education has given her a sense of self-worth. As her declaration of her future goals and ambition come in her final speech, these assertions act as the resolution to difficulties that previously shaped her life. However, while these pronouncements might be seen to mirror the graduation ceremony often found in teen films, where graduation speeches discuss the endless possibilities of the students' futures, Precious has contracted HIV and the film makes it clear that she is expected to die from the disease, as many did in the 1980s. Her plans for the future seem sadly unlikely as Precious' failing health would probably prevent her from obtaining the full education she dreams of in the limited years she has left.

Her final triumphant speech seemingly glorifies the education system and its transformative potential. This hopeful representation of course is tainted by the fact that the progressive possibilities of this institution are only realised when it is removed from the Black inner-city community. Just as Precious' heterosexual desires for love and romance are confined to fantasy, the film similarly articulates the narrative tropes of the graduation within a context that sees her ambitions confined to a dream because of her HIV-positive status. One might see this film as stripped of the hope and optimism associated with (White) Hollywood youth films. However, though Precious' future is in many ways foreclosed, her cognitive, social and emotional transformation allows her character to make peace with and learn to love herself. In this way, the film suggests that though (White and/ or middle class) education may not truly offer Precious the future she longs for, it can change how she understands her life in the here and now.

Conclusion

Precious draws on the subgenre of the school film, offering a moralising discourse where education – that is to some degree removed and disconnected from the traditional educational offerings within poor African-American communities – is presented as a means to bring about character change and development. By drawing on the youth film genre more broadly, the film plays with these tropes to separate Precious' life and perspective from the White, middle-class teens commonly found in Hollywood youth films. This generic engagement seemingly critiques the narratives of success and inclusion that White popular culture offers to young African-American girls. Yet the film's representation of romance, the saviour teacher and the institutions of the family, education and welfare, all work to progress negatives stereotypes that suggest that the poor African-American community has nothing to offer their youths, and that only through middle-class values and education can poor African-American youths escape their unstable lives. *Precious* is, consequently, a film about self-discovery and growth, as well as a film about the values of middle-class education and dysfunctional poor African-American communities.

In his account of African-American youth films, Shary argues that these films' explicit moralising often reaffirms that 'crime does not pay, staying in school is better than being on the streets, true success is measured in respect and not dollars' (2014: 42). Although *Precious* is not centrally concerned with 'street crime', it appropriates and adapts the remaining values, as the film reiterates the message that school is better than being stuck in a poor and dysfunctional African-American household, and that self-love and self-care are more important than hollow dreams of wealth, desirability and celebrity culture. While these moral positions differ from those associated with African-American male youths on screen, they nonetheless speak to middle-class positionings, through education that centres on White middle-class values and by encouraging aspirations that do not exceed a middle-class lifestyle.

3 *Precious* and narratives of girlhood (denied)

In this chapter, I investigate how *Precious* represents girlhood, depicts female maturation and makes use of age-based stereotypes, myths and norms. To begin the chapter, I first outline how narratives and myths of childhood, adolescence and adulthood have taken shape in the West. In so doing, I seek to outline how *Precious* aligns with, and more often deviates from, these socio-cultural myths. The chapter highlights how the film makes use of racial stereotypes in its depiction of Precious' maturation. I show how this use of racial stereotypes denies the main character of the maturation and development that is usually imagined for White children as they move in and through adolescence towards adulthood. Centrally, I demonstrate how the film's use of these stereotypes progresses a narrative about the abuse of a poor African-American girl and how it does not draw attention to the ways in which these stereotypes work to close down narratives that imagine the progression and development of the protagonist and African-American youths more broadly.

My discussion of Precious begins with a consideration of the concept of childhood. One might wonder why a discussion of the child is relevant when analysing a film that depicts a 16-year-old adolescent. As Precious has been sexually assaulted and abused since the age of three, her identity is at all times haunted by her childhood. This, however, is not the only reason for evaluating the figure of the child within a reading of this film. In her book *Black Children in Hollywood Cinema: Cast in Shadow* (2017) Olson considers Precious' relationship with depictions of African-American children in American culture and cinema. Admittedly, such a consideration conflates age categories as she uses 'the child', 'the adolescent' and 'girl' interchangeably. This interchangeability, while in some ways problematic, is in line with Olson's assertion that 'the stereotype of Black females as oversexed, asexual, or animalistic not only applies to adult females but also to black female children' (65), and with Griffin's argument that the controlling images of 'the mammy, jezebel, matriarch, and welfare queen,

DOI: 10.4324/9781315545547-4

foreclose[e] diverse representations of Black femininity' (2014: 183) for Black girls and women. Olson's conflation of age categories mirrors the way that African-American racial stereotypes similarly conflate age categories. While Olson is not herself concerned with unpacking the implications of the amalgamation of these age-based categories, this chapter engages with her work to draw attention to their problematic nature in narrations of African-American girlhood and maturation. This chapter's consideration of the child is in part tied to an examination of how the treatment of age norms and expectations informs the type of maturation Precious can undergo.

To make sense of the narrative of growth and maturation Precious is afforded in the film, I first outline how different age categories are largely understood within the West, before explaining how these norms and expectations are applied or denied in this coming-of-age narrative. In the West, the cultural and biological human life cycle is often divided into different age categories. These categories can vary and are often defined and redefined based on fluctuating understandings of biology and culture. Hockey and James (1993) indicate that in contemporary Western societies human development is seen to occur in an arc. It begins with infancy and transitions to childhood, which is framed as a period of innocence, development and dependency. It then moves to adolescence, which is commonly presented as a transitionary stage that moves towards adulthood. Adulthood is often marked as the pinnacle stage in the life cycle and thus the peak of the arc. It is perceived as a period of stabilisation in terms of identity as well as biological development. Finally, the arc begins to descend as middle, old and deep old age are commonly understood as a process of decline, an eventual return to dependency (i.e. a second childhood) and/or death. These categories are imbued with different cultural and biological understandings that work together, and at times in opposition, to make sense of and narrate human development.

What defines children and childhood has changed over time. Although the child is commonly described as a prepubescent person (James 2000), the age at which puberty takes place can greatly vary between people. This discursively constructed biological category is consequently at odds with some cultural perceptions of the child. As Steven Bruhm and Natasha Hurley note, while age-of-consent laws cast people under the age of 16 usually as children, 'teens who rape or murder are tried as "adults"' (2004: xxv). They conclude that 'there may very well be no definition of "child" that applies to all situations' (ibid). This fluidity of biological and cultural discourses highlights the challenge of singularly defining and classifying what a child is and when one begins and stops being a child. However, more generally, the child is understood as a prepubescent person, most commonly ranging from 3 to 12 years of age (Papalia et al. 2006: 8). Culturally, the child is thought to be innocent (primarily, sexually innocent), emotional, simplistic, natural and pure. The child is often perceived as lacking a full understanding of an adult world. These are cultural traits that emerged and became strongly connected to the child in the eighteenth century (Heywood 2001, Cunningham 1995).

This dominant understanding of the child in the West largely derives from the work of Jean-Jacques Rousseau. Rousseau rejected the idea of the 'original sin', as described in the Christian tradition. He resisted Puritan beliefs that the child needed to be strictly religiously educated to distinguish between good and evil. Instead, he believed that 'as innocents, [children] could be left to respond to nature, and then they would do nothing but good. They might cause damage, but not with the intention of doing harm' (Heywood 2001: 24). Rousseau's reimagining of the child increased society's focus on childhood and encouraged it to recognise the child as distinct from the adult. The concerns of the Enlightenment, and later the Romantic and Victorian eras, saw the formation of social systems and narratives that centred on the child's 'needs'. This increased attention meant that by the nineteenth century 'childhood had become a powerful force in middle-class Europe and North America' (Cunningham 1995: 41).

As childhood attracted increasing attention, the nature of how children developed into adults became of central concern. As Cunningham argued, at this time

> [T]he importance of childhood . . . manifested itself in . . .: . . . a belief in the importance of early education; . . . a concern for the salvation of the child's soul; . . . a growing interest in the way children learned; and . . . a sense that children were messengers of God, and that childhood was therefore the best time of life.
>
> (ibid.)

This cultural and theoretical perception of the child led to the reform of educational and religious systems, as well as child labour laws, as society increasingly sought to protect the child from the moral (and sexual) degradation of adult life.

It is through these changes that the cult of youth took shape. Cunningham argues that 'at the heart of this ideology lay . . . a conviction that the way childhood was spent was crucial in determining the kind of adult that the child would become' (ibid.). The belief that 'proper' childhoods produced functioning adults, resulted in the policing of childhood and children throughout the nineteenth century. This policing was primarily concerned with protecting children's innocence, and more specifically, their sexual innocence (Bailey 2013, also see Foucault 1978). Children were at once seen as nonsexual (free from sexual desire) and as future heteronormative subjects. As Bruhm and Hurley state, 'there is currently a dominant narrative about children: children are (and should stay) innocent of sexual desire and intentions' (2004: ix). Yet children are also assumed to be heterosexual (ibid.), with 'cute boy-girl romance read . . . as evidence for the mature sexuality that awaits them', and homoerotic behaviour framed 'as harmless play' to be later 'corrected by marriage' (ibid.). As such, in the nineteenth century, and to a large extent today, discourses on childhood innocence denied children of the very sexuality that they were expected to assume as adults. This focus on children's innocence and non-sexualised development speaks to a fear of the 'corrupted' child and the enduring belief that sexual abuse perverts the child, disrupts their maturation and leads to the formation of a dysfunctional adult (xxii). The policing of the child's innocence was and is consequently equally about the policing of adult behaviours (see also Holland 2004, Kincaid 1998).

The growing and continued concern over child welfare has resulted in the formation of four main characteristics that are attributed to the child, '(1) the child is spatially and temporally set apart as different, as "other"; (2) the child is said to have a special nature, and to be associated with nature; (3) the child is innocent and therefore (4) vulnerability dependent' (Hockey and James 1993: 60). As the idealisation of the child in the West has traditionally focused on the child's needs, it gave shape to a 'culturally legitimated "root metaphor" for dependency' that stresses the child's disabilities rather than abilities (136, 140).

As the child grows and develops towards adulthood, they are seen to enter the transitionary space of adolescence. Shary suggests that in the Early Modern period society began to recognise that there was a distinct stage between childhood and adulthood. Though the term adolescence was not commonly used, this stage was characterised by sexual maturation and a 'more complex sociopsychological manifestation of cultural and internal conflict' (Shary 2014: 20). However, it has also been argued that prior to the eighteenth century 'little psychological significance was attached to' this stage, and that '[t]he reaching of adulthood was determined by the acquisition of independence, a point [. . . that has] no direct connection with physiological maturity' (Rutter 1980: 5). It is consequently difficult to say with certainty what conception of adolescence took shape prior to the 1700s. However, by the twentieth-century adolescence was identified as a period of 'increased [or increasing] maturity and (eventual) stabilization of identity' (Driscoll 2002: 5), that was connected to puberty and the teenage years.

In a contemporary context, adolescence connotes the movement 'between dependence and independence[,] . . . between ignorance and knowledge' (Driscoll 2002: 52), and between immaturity and maturity. It is associated with physical and sexual development, as the adolescent is perceived as 'physiological[ly] differen[t] from what precedes [childhood] and follows it [adulthood]' (49). The adolescent is often associated with emotional instability and a lack of adult maturity. These connotations derive from 'the adult world['s] exaggerat[ion of] the more problematic features of adolescence, [. . . and] the negative perceptions of adolescence . . . directly caused by their [adolescents'] own behavior'(Coleman 2011: 3).

In his consideration of adolescence, Rutter outlines the conditions that gave rise to the contemporary recognition of this distinct stage of life. He argues:

> Adolescence is treated as a distinct stage of development because the coincidence of extended education and early sexual maturation have meant a prolonged phase of physical maturity associated with economic dependence; because many of the widely held psychological theories specify that adolescence should be different; because commercial interests demanded a youth culture; and because schools and colleges have ensured that large numbers of young people are kept together in an age-segregated group.
>
> (Rutter 1980: 7)

Such an account highlights the distinct institutional, social and cultural shifts that led to the recognition of adolescence more widely. Yet Rutter's views do not clearly define the specific boundaries of adolescence. As Coleman (2011: 2) questions, is adolescence marked by puberty or does the variance between when puberty occurs blur the lines of when adolescence begins? Does the performance of adolescent behaviour by younger children complicate when the transition towards adulthood occurs? Conversely, with more young adults staying at home after high school to obtain further education or to save money while working, does their continued economic dependence classify them as adolescents?

The adolescent, like the child, and like any age-based category, takes shape through competing discourses. Despite these limitations in the classification of adolescence, the adolescent might most clearly be defined as a pubescent person, between the ages of 13 and 19 years of age, who is sexually developing, and who has increasing knowledge, social awareness and (sexual) maturity. The adolescent is separated from the adult as they are not yet seen to have achieved a stabilised, independent adult identity.

While these generalised histories of the child and the adolescent are helpful as they highlight the underlining discourses, ideologies and norms that often take shape are reimagined or are reaffirmed within filmic representations of children and adolescents in the West, what is important to note is that these are White Western discourses, centrally about White Western (primarily middle- and upper-class) children and adolescents. As Olson remarks, there is a 'glaring absence of children of color in the discourse of childhood' (2017: 3). She acknowledges that the Black child is given some consideration in histories that seek to explore 'American childhoods', but even then she suggests that

> many of these histories marginalize the experiences of black children by isolating them as if they were not a part of the 'real' fabric of American society, the 'real' American childhood, but rather exist as a subculture outside historical or socio-economic mainstream of US cultural shifts.
>
> (21)

Olson suggests that on the rare occasions that Black children are brought into focus, it is usually because they have 'done, or survived, something "special"' (ibid.). Her objection to the broader general history of the child that I have detailed previously is rooted in her rightful objection to the erasure of the Black child from broader discussions of childhood and the positioning of the White (middle- to upper-class) child as the model of the ideal child and childhood, as this casts all other children as 'othered', or rather as 'nonchild' (23).

As a nonchild, African-American slave children were denied their personhood. While White children's labour and bodies were seen as in need of protection, historically, the African-American child was denied these protections, as their labour was viewed as 'natural' and because they were not viewed as persons but as property (Olson 2017: 23). As such, Olson asserts that 'the black child elided the notion of innocence altogether' (ibid.; see also Owen 2019). Although the visual depictions of Black children have changed dramatically since slavery, Olson argues 'the cultural pattern of derogatory representation of black children continues in visual portrayals in a variety of mediums today' (2017: 25). She suggests that discourses and representations of childhood through stories, songs, toys and games still locate Black children outside of the 'norm' for childhood, resulting in the absence of Black children 'from the landscape of childhood altogether' (ibid.).

If one returns to the foundational notion that children are born with an innate goodness that marks them as innocent, what we find is that while White Western childhood is commonly framed, understood and explored in relation to innocence, the Black child is divorced from the 'European innocence [that] was [and is] utopian, pure, [and] ethereal' (Olson 2017: 27). Instead, Olson argues that the Black child is connected to the '"primordial" innocence of colored peoples', an innocence that was 'tied to ignorance, lack of civilization and a lack of intelligence' (ibid.). In this view, Olson continues, 'blacks could be childish, but never children' (ibid.). By childish she is referring to the historical framing of Black people as lacking intelligence and as being 'perpetual children in need of parental "guidance"' (30). This racist framing sees the Black community rooted in a derogatory understanding of the child as dependent and undeveloped, while denying them of the utopic frames of White children as also pure and heavenly.

I outlined all these debates about childhood and adolescence because I would argue that it is the denial of not only Black children within the landscape of childhood but also their innocence within a White European frame that shapes, informs and limits the coming-of-age story in *Precious*. Coming-of-age narratives in film find their roots in the *bildungsroman* narratives. Such stories 'offer privileged access to the psychological development of a central character whose sense of self is in flux, paralleling personal concerns with prevailing values' (Graham 2019: 1). While these narratives traditionally focused on privileged, young male, Caucasian characters, increasingly in more recent years, marginalised groups have become the focus of these types of narratives (McCulloch 2019: 175–6). This includes the 'minority female bildungsroman' literary subgenre in which authors provide powerful counter-narratives where the marginalised voices of women of colour are highlighted (Michlin 2006: 181).

The *bildungsroman* was adopted within film in the shape of the coming-of-age film. Movies in this category tend to explore a character's movement from immaturity to maturity, their transition from childhood to adulthood, and their physical (and at times sexual) growth and social development. The coming-of-age narrative tends to focus on the characters' loss of innocence as they grow up. It often frames this loss as a potentially painful process (Hanson 2000: 154).

Coming-of-age and the nonchild in *Precious*

Precious is identifiable as a coming-of-age film because it focuses on a girl who learns how to survive and escape her abusive home to develop and claim her new identity as a strong, confident and independent woman. Yet, as a critical component of the coming-of-age narrative relies on a White European perception of the child as not only innocent but also as separated from the adulthood that awaits said child, Precious' coming-of-age is disjointed from this traditional narrative structure as her Black identity, and the film's alignment of her with the nonchild, problematises a reading of her development as rooted in her loss of innocence and distance from adulthood.

In *Precious*, the main character's childhood is only explored and represented in a limited way. The audience is given a sense of the heroine's childhood, and how she was treated and perceived as a (non)child through brief references made to her by her mother, through the showing of four family photos of Precious as a baby and child, by Precious' account of being pregnant two times with the age of the first child suggesting that she was 12 or 13 when she gave birth and through the depiction of other African-American children within her family and community, namely, her daughter Mongo (Quisha Powell) and her neighbour Ruby (Shayla Stewart; this character does not appear in the book).

When referring to Precious, her mother conflates the age categories of infant, child and adult as she refers to her daughter as both her baby and her child (in reference to Precious at any age), and as she also accuses Precious of being a 'big woman' and of stealing her man. Mary's framing of her daughter reveals how the latter is positioned simultaneously as a child and a woman within her own family. The mother's use of these age-based terms and descriptions, and her accounts of Precious at different ages, often serves as a means for her to control, claim ownership of and/or belittle her daughter. For instance, at the start of the film, Mary, during a tyrant of abuse, tells Precious that she 'knew it the day the doctors put [Precious] in [her] goddam hands, [Precious] wasn't a goddamn thing'. In this remark, Mary belittles her by suggesting that she never had any value. Furthermore, by asserting that her daughter 'wasn't a god damn thing', Mary denies Precious' personhood, reducing her to less than a thing. In many ways, this description of the main character reflects the way that Black children and infants were treated during slavery. As Olson argues, Black children were often denied their personhood as they were seen as objects (2017: 23). Mary's abuse of Precious thus mimics this historical abuse and treatment of Black children in the United States even when in this case the abuse is coming from a child's own mother.

Despite this early framing, the film goes on to problematise and question Mary's initial representation of Precious as lacking value. This is done through the depiction of four family photos and through Mary's account of Precious' infancy and childhood at the end of the film. During a physical fight between the two, shortly before Precious leaves Mary's household for good with her infant son, four photos are edited in. These photos depict mother and daughter when the latter was an infant and then a child. In the first two (see Figures 3.1 and 3.2), Mary is well dressed. She holds an infant Precious in her arms as they sit next to a Christmas tree. Mary looks directly and joyfully into her daughter's face as Precious does the same with her mother. It is clear from this image that there is affection and love between the two. Precious is neatly dressed, and in the second photo her hair has

Figure 3.1 Mary holding Precious as an infant

Figure 3.2 Mary and Precious' shared affection

been prettily arranged. This suggests that she is being physically and affectionately cared for during this time. This care is later reflected in Mary's description of Precious as an infant at the end of the film. She describes how her daughter was precious to her and how she had a special pillow to lie her on. These descriptions of care and the photographic images of this time counter Mary's initial claims that Precious was not anything from the time of her birth. In this way, love, innocence and purity become associated with Precious' infancy.

Following the depiction of these two photos, two additional photos are shown of Precious as a child (see Figures 3.3 and 3.4). In the first photo, mother and daughter are shown together. Neither Mary's nor Precious' hair is decoratively styled, and both wear plain clothing. As Brooks and McNair highlight, in Black culture 'combing and fixing hair provides mothers and daughters, friends, and siblings with opportunities to bond and talk about hair and other things' (2015: 305). Their un-styled hair suggests that the

Figure 3.3 Mary and Precious' growing distance

Figure 3.4 Precious' isolation in childhood

characters are no longer bonding with one another and are isolated from each other and their broader community. In contrast to the earlier photos, Mary is wearing neither makeup nor earrings. Furthermore, Precious is overweight, which suggests that the abuse inflicted on her through both starvation and then over feeding (as depicted during her teen years) is already taking place. This implies that Mary is no longer caring for either her daughter or herself, and that Precious is likely now being abused. Where in the earlier photos the two look affectionately at one another, in this photo, Precious sits on the floor at a distance from her mother, who is seen lowering herself into an armchair with her body turned away from her daughter. Precious is no longer smiling, and she stares blankly at the camera. Finally, in the last photo a child Precious is shown in the image by herself, sat under a Christmas tree. Her face is blank, and she stares out somewhere beyond the camera. She is now depicted as both isolated from her mother and from those who are around her, as symbolised by her lack of engagement with the person taking the photo. What these photos suggest is that as she becomes a child, she begins to be abused, and she loses the love and innocence she had as an infant.

The suggestion of childhood abuse these photos point towards is reaffirmed at the end of the film when Mary relates that Carl began to sexually abuse Precious when she was three. As indicated previously, while what defines childhood is in flux, the age range commonly associated with the child is between the ages of 3 and 12. As Precious' abuse occurs at the moment that she is no longer an infant but a child, Precious never experiences childhood's sexual innocence as her early abuse sees her sexual innocence confined to infanthood. Precious is consequently positioned as a nonchild as her sexual knowledge sees her distanced from European childhood innocence and its ties to purity, and as her sexual abuse sees her treated as an object.

Representing female children in *Precious*

Precious' nonchild status, while briefly explored through the intersection between the family photos and Mary's accounts, is reaffirmed through the treatment of other Black children in the film. While Precious gives birth to a baby boy, there are only two children (between the ages of 3 and 12) depicted in the film, and both are girls. One is Precious' daughter Mongo, and the other is her neighbour Ruby. Although little time is spent depicting Mongo, she nonetheless becomes a marker of childhood abuse and of the nonchild. Firstly, Mongo serves as the physical evidence of her mother's childhood abuse. As Precious is 16 at the start of the film, and her daughter is around the age of three or four, Mongo's age suggests that Precious was 12 or 13 when she had her, and thus likely between the ages of 11 and 13 when she became pregnant. When read in line with the book, in which Precious asserts that she is 12 when she has Mongo, it suggests that the main character was likely 11 or 12 when she was impregnated. Mongo thus serves as evidence of Precious' robbed innocence, her treatment as a sexual object and her abuse during childhood.

Mongo and Precious are further linked through their relationship with Mary. For example, when Precious first registers for Each One Teach One, her alternative school, she is asked about her financial situation. The audience learns that Mary collects money for both her daughter and granddaughter, and that both are on Mary's 'budget'. As Mongo does not live with Precious and Mary, it becomes clear that she is functioning as a 'meal ticket' for her grandmother, and that the money collected is being used for the latter's benefit rather than for the care of Mongo. As Mongo's and Precious' financial relationship with Mary is revealed at the same time, like her daughter, Precious is and has been seemingly functioning as an economic resource for Mary. In this way, they both reflect the way that, historically, the Black child lived their lives as property and were treated as objects of economic rather than personal value. Mary's financial use of her daughter and granddaughter sees them reduced to property (a point she reaffirms at the end of the film when she insists on a reunion with her daughter and grandchildren under the rationale that they 'belong to' her).

Mary verbally abuses Mongo, referring to her as an 'animal'. While her use of vocabulary may reflect her prejudice against her granddaughter who has Down's syndrome, as Mongo is also a child, her choice of words denies her the innocence that is commonly afforded to White middle- and upper-class children in the West. Instead, she connects Mongo with the '"primordial," innocence of colored peoples' that Olson argued about (2017: 27), in which they are framed as uncivilised. As Mongo is only one of two children depicted in the film, this labelling of her holds greater weight and sees the film connect Black children more broadly to racist framings of African-American people's 'innocence'.

The other child the film introduces is Ruby. Olson tells us, 'historically, black children were rarely visualised as occupying "childhood" spaces like the nursery or playroom' (2017: 33). She suggests that these spaces, as spaces of play and innocence, were reserved for White children, and that they excluded children of colour, who were not seen as able to inhabit these spaces in the same way. Similarly, we never see Ruby within a childhood space. She is instead featured in the alleyway outside the flats, inside the stairwell and in the waiting room in the welfare office. She is primarily alone, with one exception where she is seen with her mother. She is never depicted playing with other children. Ruby has a limited number of lines in the film, but from her interaction with Precious it is clear that she is neither cared for nor does she inhabit the space of childhood. For example, when Ruby is first introduced, she asks Precious when they are going to play. Standing in an alleyway, she does not inhabit a space that we might recognise as safe for child play. Her only potential object for this play is a doll she carries with her. The doll is naked, and its arms are missing. The damaged state of the doll and its positioning within an alley full of garbage gives the impression that this is a discarded doll Ruby has discovered rather than a toy brought out from a child's play space. Furthermore, as the doll is Caucasian, the play that is possible with this doll seems limited to a White Western frame, which, because Ruby is a Black child, she is always already excluded from. Ruby's request to play with Precious is unsurprisingly rejected, as a 16-year-old is unlikely to look for friendship or wish to play the same games as a child. Nonetheless, the request serves to highlight her isolation from other children and from child spaces as she looks for friendships among adolescent girls.

Ruby, like Precious, is an abused child. This is apparent through her lack of supervision and through bruising around her eye. While it is not clear whether Ruby is being sexually assaulted or singularly physically abused, her bruised eye highlights her distance from childhood innocence and the utopia often associated with this period of life. Ruby is a clear victim of poverty, and this victimhood sees her further distanced from the figure of the child. For example, when Ruby is first introduced, she wears an adult-sized brown vest that comes down to her knees. On the one hand, this over-sized clothing emphasises her small size. However, on the other hand, it suggests that her child status has been overlooked, as those who are providing for her have failed to identify her needs as a child (i.e. her need to wear appropriate (child-sized) clothing). The wearing of this adult clothing positions the audience to identify her poverty, but it also highlights her neglected childhood and ignored child status. Little care has also been taken in her appearance as her hair is not neatly styled or ornamented. Like Precious, her lack of styled hair suggests her isolation from both her mother and a broader community of African-American women. She is seemingly left to care for herself. In this way, the protections normally afforded to the child are not afforded to Ruby, and the lack of care shown for her sees her given a level of independence that does not reflect the needs of the child, who is normally framed as vulnerable and dependent.

While the book spends significantly more time considering Precious' childhood, within the film the incorporation of Ruby as a new character within the storyline can be seen to represent the child Precious was and which the film does not explore in detail. This becomes particularly apparent in Ruby's final scene. Sitting in the welfare office waiting room with her mother, Ruby sits looking downcast and uncomfortable. Her mother does not seem to want to engage with her, and when she does, does so gruffly. As Ruby's mother leaves to speak to the welfare officer, she remarks to Ruby about staying put so that she can see the welfare officer before her 'shit gets cut off'. As the audience has already learned about how Mongo and Precious serve as a financial resource for Mary through her claims within the welfare system, Ruby's mother's comments about welfare and Ruby's presence at the welfare office suggest that Ruby is similarly used by her mother for money. Her lack of proper clothing, the little care taken in her appearance and her social isolation and neglect all suggest that this money is not being used to care for Ruby. Ruby comes to be another Black child who is used as an object/economic resource and is not recognised as a person.

Her connection to Precious as an abused child is further reaffirmed when Precious, having witnessed this exchange between Ruby and Ruby's mother, performs an act of caring by taking off her own scarf and tying it around Ruby's neck. This scarf is symbolic of Precious' journey of self-discovery and her escape from her own victimisation. By giving this scarf to Ruby, she recognises their shared experience of trauma and foreshadows the journey that Ruby will need to go on as she grows and ages. As the two characters are connected, their histories as abused and neglected children are aligned. Furthermore, as Precious is given this scarf at the start of the film, her passing of the scarf to Ruby suggests that she is relaying a symbolic torch, with each generation of African-American girls having to find their own way forward after years of abuse. In this way, both characters become symbolic of all African-American girls, because of the way their stories align and because we never see any African-American children who are living alternative lives or who are viewed and treated differently.

Girlhood, womanhood and African-American stereotyping

The framing of Precious and the other African-American children in the film as nonchildren does not invite the audience to question this stereotype. Instead, the film uses this stereotype to invite the audience to feel sympathy for these children. This is evident because while viewers are prompted to feel outraged at Mary's abuse and triumph at Precious' courage, they are not invited to question why Precious' abuse has not led to intervention and why adults around her are not concerned about her lack of childhood innocence. For example, it is striking that though Precious' principal and her welfare officer remark about her having two children, they never highlight or discuss the fact that she was a child when she was impregnated with her first child. As a nonchild Precious is already seemingly distanced from a European understanding of innocence. As Olson (2017) suggests, Black female children are often associated with stereotypes that are also associated with Black adulthood, like the figure of the jezebel. The jezebel is framed as a hypersexual African-American woman. In this respect, one could argue that as the Black child is distanced from the European child and connected to stereotypes that reflect adult roles and positions, the Black child is positioned in a racist manner as not in need of protection from sex as they are perceived as already sexual. This argument would align with Dagbovie-Mullins' contention that 'representations of black girlhood in the media and popular culture suggest that black girls face a different set of rules when it comes to sex, innocence and blame' (2013: 764).

Just as Precious' high-school principal does not seek to question or discuss Precious' first pregnancy, her response to Precious that this is now her second pregnancy and her question 'what happened?' verbalises the principal's disappointment that the student is pregnant again. Rather than questioning how a minor has been impregnated twice and seeking to hold other parties responsible for this unlawful situation, the principal's disappointment and the way she ascribes blame to the main character reflect the 'tendency [in America] to view black adolescent females as sexually savvy and therefore responsible themselves for the sexualization and exploitation of their bodies' (Dagbovie-Mullins 2013: 746). This stereotypical framing of Black female sexuality sees Precious denied of the concern, support and protection that should otherwise be afforded to her as a minor. As the film never highlights Precious' child status when she conceived her first child, the audience is not invited to critique the principal's assumption that she was and is sexualised. Nor are they invited to question the principal's consequential positioning of Precious' child and adolescent self as a jezebel, a label that would be all too adult for a White child. Similarly, the audience is not prompted to question the positioning of Precious as a nonchild by her social worker, who at no point contacts child services about Precious' abuse, despite her status as a minor. In other words, the film uses the positioning of the Black child as nonchild to create sympathy for Precious' plight but does not seek to question the way the society's framing of the Black child as nonchild sees them denied of the rights and privileges that would protect and prevent the type of abuse depicted in the film.

In terms of narrative structure and arc, the positioning of Precious as a nonchild during her childhood directly shapes the limits of the coming-of-age narrative that is afforded to her. When she is first introduced on screen, the markers of her childhood self are already gone. In many ways, she is also already visually and culturally separated from the figure of the adolescent. In casting the actress Gabourey Sidibe, who, at the age of 26, had already outgrown her own adolescence, the character of Precious becomes embodied by an obese adult rather than the still developing body of an obese teen. Furthermore, her treatment by figures of authority, her community and her mother serve to repeatedly frame her as an adult, despite her status as a 16-year-old girl.

Indeed, other characters refer to her by using terms that are associated with adulthood, with a boy in her neighbourhood referring to her as 'big mamma', and her mother referring to her as a 'rival', on account of Carl having given Precious more children than he has given Mary. In both cases, Precious' sexuality is used to associate her with adulthood. The term 'mamma' connects her to a matured and stereotyped sexuality associated with Black womanhood, as the mother who has given birth is always already sexed. Furthermore, as the term is associated with the image of the caring mother, this usage thus positions her not as a dependent in need of care but as a carer. Similarly, Mary's accusations are that Precious has 'stolen' her man, paints the two characters as rivals and equals rather than as mother and daughter. This accusation sees Mary align Precious with the figure of the jezebel, whose hypersexual nature associates her with an adult sexuality. Finally, her pregnant body reaffirms her positioning outside of adolescence as she is not in the process of discovering her sexuality but rather in the process of rediscovering motherhood.

The public institutions that seek to engage with Precious also largely treat her as an adult. For example, after Precious is kicked out of school, she is instructed by her mother to 'get herself down to the welfare'. When at the welfare, Precious is treated as an adult rather than as an adolescent. This is seen through the way she obtains funds to support herself. As she is no longer enrolled in a traditional school, she is seen to have entered the adult world. As such, when it is clear that she is being abused, no effort is made to contact child services, despite the fact that she is not yet 18. Furthermore, rather than seeking to support her education, the welfare state treats her as a financial drain and encourages her to work, that is, to become 'independent'. The film presents a critical framing of the work she is offered. However, the criticisms presented centre around the way this type of work will serve to keep her in poverty and isolate her from her child, rather than considering the way that the acceptance of this type of work would see her enter the responsibilities of adulthood. Although narratives of adolescence often focus on self-discovery and development, despite a continuing degree of dependency, this dependency is usually confined within the family structure rather than within the state. Precious, while undergoing self-discovery and development, is not simply dependent on her family but is rather dependent on the state. As she is not depicted as a child of the state, her increasing dependency on it becomes an adult dependency. This reflects the way that African Americans are often framed as childish in terms of their dependency, without being children.

The film rarely reaffirms Precious' status as an adolescent. Nonetheless, her adolescence is depicted through both her fanciful daydreams, which point to her struggle to make sense of her place within the world and to come to terms with and escape from her trauma, and Ms. Rain's remarks about Precious' young age. Although Ms. Rain is seemingly unsure of how old Precious is, first reminding Precious that she is only 17 and later asserting that she is 16, she nonetheless identifies Precious as a teenager. Furthermore, in encouraging Precious to stay in school, she reaffirms the need for Precious' further growth and development. Thus, while Precious' adolescent status is repeatedly denied by her narrative arc and by other characters in the film, viewers are fleetingly reminded that she is in fact an adolescent.

This slippery depiction of Precious as at times a woman and at times an adolescent is perhaps unsurprising. Though the film makes use of a coming-of-age narrative, its framing of Precious as a nonchild inhibits linear depictions of her growth. The main character's adolescence cannot function as a space of physical and sexual development as she has already been faced with the moral and sexual 'degradation' of adulthood, and because she has repeatedly been denied her personhood. On the other hand, as the film explores her personal growth when she moves towards a stabilised and confident adult identity, the framing of adolescence as a transitionary moment before adulthood is in some ways facilitated by the film. What this suggests is that within this coming-of-age narrative, Precious' nonchild status inhibits the possibility of reading coming-of-age in this Black girlhood narrative as one of physical and sexual maturation. The movement away from innocence cannot occur in this narrative as the Black girl has already been denied this positioning. As such, the only coming-of-age that can be afforded to this Black girl is one of emotional growth and the stabilisation of identity.

One might assume that as Precious moves towards adulthood, she is realigned with a White Western framing of this stage as the pinnacle in human development and in the lifecycle. On the surface, the film initially gives this impression of progression towards and secureness of a stabilised adulthood. After all, Precious manages to escape her abusive home, progresses in her schooling and learns to love herself. Yet the framing of her as a nonchild in childhood, that is, a child who has not been protected and afforded the (sexual) innocence of the White Western child, sees the narrative trajectory of Precious mirror the narrative of the corrupted child detailed in White Western myths of the child. It is through a consideration of this mirroring that it becomes clear that Precious' nonchild status inhibits her movement towards a stabilised adulthood.

As Bruhm and Hurley have argued, in Western narratives, a corrupted child is seen to be tainted (2004: xxii). Rather than growing into functioning members of an adult society, in narratives of the corrupted child these children become dysfunctional adults. Furthermore, Bruhm and Hurley suggest that in narratives where the child is corrupted by sexual abuse, this abuse is often destructive, leading ultimately to the death of the child (xiii-xiv). Like the corrupted child, as a nonchild Precious' narrative follows a similar trajectory. As her innocence is denied to her because it has been corrupted by sexual abuse, this brings her to destruction before she can reach adulthood. This occurs as we learn that Precious has contracted HIV from her father. As there was no cure for HIV in the 1980s, this prognosis is a death sentence. Thus, while the film ends on a somewhat uplifting note with Precious recognising her own value, coming to terms with her mother's abusive behaviour, and seeking to act independently as a mother by reclaiming both her children and by moving away from the welfare system, as she is already dying from HIV, the adulthood she is seemingly moving towards is a period of decline rather than stabilisation. As her prognosis means she will likely only have a few years to live, the lifecycle is cut short for the protagonist. In this way, the promise of stabilisation found in the coming-of-age narrative is not open to Precious. Her nonchild status and the way this status mirrors the narrative trajectory of the corrupted child inhibit the traditional development seen in coming-of-age narratives.

Conclusion

What this chapter has demonstrated is how the separation of the Black child from White childhood innocence limits the types of narratives about development and coming-of-age that are possible for the Black girl within *Precious*. The Black child's nonchild status means that racial stereotypes rather than childhood innocence frame how this child can be read and understood within the film. The film's use of these stereotypes, while intended to create sympathy for the plight of Precious and other Black children like her, nonetheless inhibits coming-of-age narratives that are based on a linear sense of progression and development. Instead, the narrative is reduced to a story of decline and degradation. These stereotypical framings of Black children highlight the way that the treatment of Black children during slavery continues to haunt the way Black girlhood is narrated within a contemporary American film. Furthermore, they show how the nonchild status facilitates a blurring of age categories, and how this blurring limits the types of stories about growth, development and decline that are afforded to the young heroine. Without the clear divisions between child, adolescent, adult and middle/old age, Precious is denied that arc of development that is afforded to White children within broader myths of White Western childhood and coming-of-age.

4 *Precious'* critical reception and the landscape of colour-blind racism

This chapter considers how *Precious* was critically received by the popular press. It analyses 36 articles and film reviews from 29 different newspapers and magazines. Many scholars (Maltby 2007, Staiger 1992, Kredell 2018, De Silva 1998, Jedidi et al. 1998, Litman and Ahn 1998, Ravid 1999, Sochay 1994, Jancovich 2001, Klinger 1994, Bode 2010) who make use of the so-called satellite texts, like film reviews, as their primary source of analysis argue about how a film was understood by audiences. They focus on how film reviews may have helped to inform understandings of genre conventions, explore how articles and film reviews may predict a film's commercial success/failure or contribute to the creation/perpetuation of hierarchies of taste. Useful as these areas of focus are when contemplating how a film may connect with audiences, they do not constitute the aims and considerations of this chapter. They provide, however, a relevant base to alternatively explore how *Precious* functions as a platform through which one could implicitly or explicitly engage with, question or reaffirm the social norms and values that were dominant in U.S. society when the film was released. This chapter highlights the socio-cultural and socio-historic frames in which *Precious* was received. These considerations draw attention to how the ideologies, stereotypes, values and norms found in *Precious*, as they have been discussed thus far, find resonance or dissonance with the ideologies, stereotypes, values and norms circulated more broadly within Western media at the time.

The chapter is structured around four key sections. The first section highlights how satellite texts have been analysed and understood by scholars, and explains how the chapter's theoretical and methodological approach links with traditions of historical reception in film studies. The second section provides a broad overview of the critical response to the film, while the final two sections, respectively, evaluate the use of a universalising discourse and discussions of race that take shape in these reviews. As the body of this chapter demonstrates, despite the film's narrative positioning within

DOI: 10.4324/9781315545547-5

the late 1980s, the critical response to *Precious* gives voice to the dynamic, and at times contradictory, racial politics of the Obama era (2008–2016). Indeed, the critical reception of the film highlights the fragility of Black identities and communities in the late 2000s as the reviews and articles engage in colour-blind discourses, seek to rationalise, challenge or perpetuate stereotypes connected to the Black community and/or draw attention to the divided response of the Black community to the film.

Reading and analysing film reviews: a methodological consideration

In the 1980s and 1990s, media scholars sought to move away from a discussion of an ideal spectator – one created by and reflected in an expert academic reading of a text. Film scholars who were interested in how audiences engage with and understand media texts began taking an ethnographic approach by using focus groups or interviews (Stokes 2001: 6–8). For scholars seeking to understand a film's historical reception, this type of ethnographic work had obvious limitations. For example, audiences who watched the film at its release might have limited or inaccurate memories of the event, might have been few in numbers or might no longer be alive. Due to these constraints, scholars turned to written materials published at the film's release, especially film reviews and press articles, to gain insight into how a film was possibly received within particular historical and geographical contexts.

Yet, as Barker points out, reviews also take 'place for quite specific purposes – and to be a writer of reviews is to be one particular kind of audience' (2004). This suggests that these paratexts do not contain the 'pure', unaffected response of an audience member reflecting on their film watching experience, but a structured and mediated response. Early reception studies scholars such as Staiger (1992) and Erb (1998) questioned the validity of using film reviews and press articles to assess a film's historical reception because they reflect this mediated rather than unaffected response. Yet arguments about scholars' abilities to access a 'pure' response to a film are difficult to defend, as every person's reading of a text is in some way determined by the ideological and institutional structures that inform their worldview and, as Barker ultimately goes on to highlight, all viewing practices are mediated. Regardless, the recognition of mediated viewership enabled scholars to begin to unpack the function of film reviews and other satellite texts within the broader reception of a film, creating a framework through which such texts can become useful in academic film engagement.

Specifically, scholars began to consider the placement of film reviews within the broader 'flow of talk around a film' (Barker 2004). As reviews served the function of critiquing and assessing the value of a film for their reader, it would be easy to consider how these texts seek to tell audiences what to think about a given film. Contemplating the role of film critics, Bode suggests that '[. . . they] perform an important role in pre-shaping audience reception' (2010: 708) and, quoting Pierre Bourdieu, she aligns with his argument stating that critics 'influence ideas of "what is worthy of being seen" what is unworthy, and "the right way to see it"' (Bourdieu, quoted in ibid.). While one might read Bode's assertion within the framework of the hypodermic needle model, scholars such as Barbara Klinger (1994: 70) and Robert C. Allen and Douglas Gomery (1985: 90) argue that film reviews highlight what audiences may wish to contemplate about a film, rather than telling audiences directly what to think about it. Framing film reviews in this way enables scholars to evade a hypodermic needle model of thinking and instead consider the agenda-setting function of film reviews. It also helps scholars to build on Bourdieu's (1984) ideas about cultural taste formation and consider how the agenda-setting function of film reviews can play a role in creating hierarchies of cultural taste. Considering the film reviewer's role in taste formation, Jancovich writes:

> Any review, or any other act of criticism, is in itself 'an affirmation of its own legitimacy', a claim by the reviewer of his or her entitlement to participate in the process by which cultural value is defined and distinguished, and thus to take part not only in a legitimate discourse about the film, but also in the production of its cultural value.
>
> (2001: 37)

In exploring critics' use of such legitimatising discourses in their film reviews, scholars like Jancovich and Klinger (1994) suggest that critics function as gatekeepers who invite audiences to position themselves within the hierarchies of taste the critics have established.

While many scholars have been concerned with how the agenda-setting function of reviews facilitates hierarchies of taste, I am not particularly concerned in this chapter with how film reviews invite the audience to read and interpret *Precious* based on taste. I do however think that the exploration of film reviews as agenda-setting texts and as texts of historical significance are productive avenues for the type of analysis I plan to undertake. I am consequently interested in considering other ways that film reviews can be read for their agenda-setting function, particularly in terms of the ideological positions that the reviews of *Precious* seem to perpetuate.

I am not alone in this interest. Scholars who have studied the relationship between film reviews and race, such as Hughey (2010, 2014) and Anderson and Grether (2017), have also sought to explore how film reviews give insights into the ideologies and norms that are dominant at a film's release.

Anderson and Grether in particular highlight that while scholars have long argued that 'portrayals of blacks in films perpetuate long-standing racial stereotypes', little attention has been given to how film reviews respond to these racial portrayals (2017: 108). Following Kim et al. (2002), Anderson and Grether assert that 'it is critical to pay close attention to how racial stereotypes are perceived by media outlets because they, in turn, help to shape the climate of racial understanding and interaction in the United States' (2017: 108). This is a particular kind of work that is greatly needed. However, although I share Anderson and Grether's interest in the ideological frames found within film reviews, the goals of this chapter are somewhat different as my analysis brings together an understanding of film reviews of *Precious* as *both* agenda-setting texts *and* historical documents that give insight into the racial discussions and debates which *Precious* instigated, and which it was surrounded by.

In doing this, my work is more aligned with Matthew Hughey's (2014) approach and consideration of film reviews and questions of race. Hughey argues that scholars often ignore how film reviews narrow the potential readings of a film. As he puts it:

> By tackling this side of the equation, we can enter the circuit of meaning by asking how the polysemy of film is settled through the labor of film critics, not as atomistic and disconnected actors, but as a coherent interpretive community, itself influenced by the dominant discourse and imperatives of current race relations.
>
> (2014: 75)

Hughey draws attention to two important points here. Firstly, he highlights the way film reviews take shape and are influenced by the broader norms, values and ideologies found in a community at the time of the review. Secondly, he invites readers to contemplate how the limiting of the polysemic meanings of a film reveals the agenda-setting function of film reviews, as they direct their reader to the ideas or points that the critic feels the reader may wish to think about. In perceiving film critics as individuals deeply enmeshed in society rather than as 'singular entities above the fray of culture' (ibid.), one can recognise the way that critics' discourse engages with and reflects dominant perceptions found at the time of a film's release. More specifically, in terms of race, their alignment with or challenge to 'commonsense' understandings of race can give insight into the racial ideologies and discourses that were present at the time of their writing.

As one considers the way film reviews narrow meaning and invites particular readings of a film, one can unpack how discourses surrounding race are refined, challenged or perpetuated. Scholars can explore how audiences were *invited* to understand a film within the broader values of a particular community. *Precious* is a film that is centrally informed by a consideration of race. In examining the way film reviews and press articles invite particular readings of the film, the chapter highlights what discourses around race were circulating at the time of the film's release and therefore informing its reception. Furthermore, as the chapter considers the agenda-setting function of these reviews, it outlines what ideologies and values film reviews invited audiences to engage with via conscious acceptance, unconscious acceptance or rejection of the values, norms and racial discourses presented in the film.

To undertake this work, I collected 36 film reviews and press articles written on *Precious* during its circulation on the film festival circuit and after its theatrical release. These reviews were written by North American and British critics. Samples were found by searching on the Business Source Complete database and by searching for reviews on Rotten Tomatoes by 'Top Critics'.[1] I was not able to access all the reviews written on *Precious* as some reviews had been removed from their web pages or are behind paywalls. I consequently selected texts that were publicly available. These publications were derived from 29 sources.[2] I first read each of these reviews to assess how *Precious* was perceived. As I read these reviews, topics covered in the reviews and press articles were noted. Some of these topics included discussions of race and the African-American community more specifically, efforts to define the film as one with a universal appeal, the struggle of Lee Daniels to produce the film, debates about the status of education in the United States and discussions of dysfunctional home lives. I went back through each review and press article and identified any quotations that corresponded to these topics. I kept a tally of how many articles engaged with identified topics. In this chapter, I analyse how the selected texts engage with these topics in relation to the film. Such analysis draws on cultural studies and specifically contemplates how scholarship on colour-blind discourses gives insight into the broader social discussions these articles generate as they seek to make sense of *Precious*.

An overview of *Precious'* critical reception

Precious largely received positive reviews. Twenty-one of the articles recommended viewers watch the film and/or celebrated its success as a compelling film and/or on the film festival/awards circuits. Of the remaining articles, three were negative, six provided no recommendation either way and eight were mixed in their assessment of the film. The reviews commonly reflected on the challenging nature of the film. For example, Orr in the *New Republic* wrote, 'that material so grim has been rendered watchable, let alone a forceful cinematic experience, is a testament to director

Lee Daniels and, especially, his cast' (2009), while, writing for *Newsweek*, Kelley highlighted that '*Precious* is not an easy movie to watch' (2009: 61) and *Rolling Stone*'s Travers succinctly summarised the difficult material the film engages with:

> When I tell people how good this movie is – and I can't shut up about it – they flash me the stink eye. As in 'Yeah, right, like I need to sink into a depression coma for two hours watching a fat, illiterate, HIV-positive Harlem girl get knocked up (twice) by her daddy, brutally battered by her mother and laughed at by a world eager to pound abuse on her 16-year-old ass'.
>
> (2009)

These reviews tend to put the difficulty of the film's content front and centre. Daniels' ability to make what would be perceived as otherwise unwatchable content viewable is one of the central ways reviews of the film praise its success. Within this discourse, the film was described by critics in vivid ways as 'heart wrenching', a 'healing touchstone', 'inspirational', 'harrowing', 'depressing', 'monstrous', 'horrific' and 'bleak'.

The film's success was occasionally measured through a comparison with *Slumdog Millionaire* (Boyle, 2008) (Johnson 2009: 70). This comparison focused on both films' ability to give voice to an underdog, their similar emphasis on child abuse and the ethnic 'Other', their shared success on the film festival circuit and their predicted and actual success at the Oscars. While both films separately faced criticisms for their stereotypical depictions of race and poverty, these similarities were not pointed towards in any reviews that sought to connect the two films. The reviews consequently invite us to read this comparison singularly as a measure of *Precious'* success.

The comparison to *Slumdog Millionaire* is particularly interesting in terms of how it invites viewers to watch *Precious* in relation to race. In reviews that criticised *Slumdog Millionaire*, critics argued that the film promoted a White Western colonial view of the poor in India, and that the celebration of the film in many reviews overlooked, and as a result masked, this colonial framework (see Kim 2009, Gupta 2009, Sheth and Bellman 2009, Thottam 2009: 52). As I demonstrate in the body of my analysis, a racial frame that privileges a White Western perspective is also often used when describing *Precious*. In comparing *Precious* to *Slumdog Millionaire* in a celebratory manner, some critics seemingly invite their readers to similarly overlook the racism and White Western framework that can be found in Daniels' film, in the same way that the majority of reviews of *Slumdog Millionaire* invited audiences to celebrate and view the film from a White Western perspective.

Precious' underdog narrative was a common focus in the majority of the film reviews and press articles. Reviewers focused primarily on *Precious'* narrative of self-discovery and transformation, although two press articles sought to highlight the underdog status of the film in terms of production (Longwell 2009, Schuker 2009). In these two pieces, attention was drawn to the unlikelihood of Hollywood financing a film like *Precious*, with Longwell from the *Hollywood Reporter* stating, 'Because the subject matter – an obese teen, pregnant for the second time by her father, seeks to escape her abusive mother – made studio backing out of the question he [Daniels] decided to forgo traditional Hollywood sources' (2009: 8–9). While Longwell suggests that Hollywood would not make a film about an obese teen, raped and abused by her parents, mainstream U.S. media had not steered entirely clear of such controversial material. Indeed, 13 years before *Precious* was released, Showtime Networks, a subsidiary of Warner-Amex Satellite Entertainment, had produced the made-for-television film *Bastard out of Carolina* (Huston, 1996), a film about a poor girl named Bone, who is physically abused, sexually molested and raped by her step-father. Her mother is aware of this abuse but refuses to leave her husband. Unlike *Precious*, however, Bone is not obese in the film, she is raped by a step-father rather than a biological parent and her mother is not a wholly despicable character. Bone is also white, which suggests that perhaps it is not so much the nature of the storyline that was at stake in *Precious* but the fact that such a storyline involves a black obese teenage girl, which makes it difficult to sensationalise and market.

Despite both articles' focus on the unlikelihood of Hollywood financing a film like *Precious*, neither article critiques Hollywood's resistance to financing films about African-American girls and women. In fact, Schuker in the *Wall Street Journal* goes as far as to rationalise Hollywood's lack of interest in films like *Precious* by stating:

> In today's cash-starved Hollywood, where the billions Wall Street poured into Hollywood between 2004 and 2008 have dried up, individual 'angel' investors like the Magnesses are more crucial than ever – and one of the only ways that gritty, independent films like 'Precious' ever live to see the silver screen.
>
> (2009)

Such remarks seem to suggest that Hollywood's restricted finances inhibited gritty independent films from being produced. However, Schuker ignores the fact that Hollywood rarely depicts African-American girlhood on screen, let alone an obese, sexually abused and poor African-American girl in a leading role. As late as 2011, it was determined that only 10.5%

of people of colour were cast in leading roles, which was well below proportional representation, and only 12.2% of people of colour were film directors (Turner and Nilsen 2019: 5). Furthermore, considering that at the same time that *Precious* was produced, *Avatar* was financed to the tune of $237,000,000, it seems unlikely that Hollywood was financially unable to finance a film costing around $10,000,000 to make.[3] In fact, Guerrero argues that:

> Hollywood has known about the disproportionately large black movie going audience since the early 1950s' and that 'the movie industry routinely ignores black filmic aspirations and marginalises black box office power until it can be called on, as a sort of reserve audience, to make up sinking profit margins at any given moment of economic crisis.
>
> (1993: 3)

If Hollywood was being selective in its funding of films because of economic deficiency as Schuker suggests, it is likely that Hollywood, as it has done in the past, would have sought to produce films targeted towards Black audiences to make up their profit margins. Writing well before the production of *Precious*, Guerrero notes:

> Studio executives figure that black-focused films are a lucrative venture as long as they are cheaply made. The current production cost for bringing in a 'small film' is anywhere from $1.5 to $10 million, and the top end of this range is about a third of what the average commercial film costs. Thus Hollywood makes these modestly budgeted black features with the expectation of recovering the capital invested and turning a profit from the black audience alone.
>
> (1993: 4)

Despite the fact that these figures are from the early 1990s, when a cycle of commercially successful ghetto-focused films revealed that there was indeed a substantial Black audience, it seems unlikely the production cost margins decreased in the 2000s. Indeed, Black-focused films like *Ray* (Hackford, 2004; Universal Pictures, $40,000,000), *Antwone Fisher* (Washington, 2002; Fox Searchlight Pictures, $12,500,000), *Why Did I Get Married* (Perry, 2007; Lions Gate Films, $15,000,000) and *Barbershop* (Gray, 2002; MGM, $12,000,000) were, according to IMDb,[4] all financed in excess of the $1.5-$10 million range that Guerrero noted in 1993.

Precious was a film that fell within the production costs of Black-focused films in the early 2000s and that engaged with hard-hitting topics, such as rape and violence, that had been depicted on screen before. However, the film differs in its portrayal as these topics are explored through the prism of an obese, poor, African-American girl. When looking at feature films released between 2000 and 2009 on IMDb (excluding *Precious*), 27 of these films sought to engage with African-American culture and communities, were biopics and/or told stories about historical African-American figures. While other films cast African Americans (primarily men), these films tended to position the African-American actor within a White community, to deal with problems that largely seemed to affect that community or a family within it. African-American females cast in these types of films often undertook supporting roles. Of the 27 films mentioned previously, 19 films centrally focused on male actors, three films centrally focused on female actors, four films co-starred male and female African-American actors (usually romantically), and one film did not prominently feature Black actors at all, but instead stereotypically depicted understandings of Black culture in New Orleans through a storyline about two African-American servants who used hoodoo to inhabit the body of White people. Of the films that featured female actors in central roles, only one was about girlhood (*Akeelah and the Bee* 2006). When looking at Rotten Tomatoes' 100 top-rated African-American films in the twenty-first century, 25 U.S. films were listed between the period 2000 and 2009. Of these films, three depicted Black girlhood (*Our Song*, 2001; *Akeelah and the Bee*, 2006; and *The Heart of the Game*, 2005). What this suggests is that the difficulty of making *Precious* may not simply reflect Hollywood's financial struggles or the film's gritty subject matter, but rather a resistance in Hollywood to depict Black girlhood, a subject that neither of these reviews sought to directly address.

While most of the reviews and press articles praised the film, reviews that were mixed or negative in their assessment tended to fall into two camps. The first perceived the film as exploitative, sought to highlight its stereotypical depiction of the 'welfare queen' and dysfunctional African-American homes and/or associated it with 'poverty porn' (Stevens 2009, Orr 2009, Lumenick 2009). These reviewers (and Morris 2009) often felt that the film reinforced racial preferences for light-skinned African Americans and the vilification of dark-skinned African Americans. The second group saw the film as hyperbolic, as too forceful in its symbolism and in some cases found fault with either Paula Patton's role as the stereotypical angelic teacher or Gabourey Sidibe's limited facial expressions due to her obesity (Lane 2009, Ross 2009, Bradshaw 2009, Edelstein 2009, Rainer 2009, Gilbey 2009). Finally, a small number of reviews seemed to be rooted in racism (Ross 2009, Bradshaw 2009, Lane 2009, Morris 2009, Mondello 2009), as I will discuss further in my analysis later.

While not all reviews approach the film from the same perspective, there were some key agendas that were shared or debated among them. These included whether the film could be read as having a universal message/story or whether this was specific to an African-American experience; whether or not the film was a call to action in regard to education, social reform or the treatment of African-American citizens; and whether the film accurately reflected the African-American experience or provided stereotypical and regressive representations. By examining the treatment of these issues and investigating the reviews' agenda-setting function, I seek to demonstrate how *Precious* becomes a platform to give voice to or challenge a colour-blind discourse.

Precious' universal appeal

Precious casts in all its leading roles African-American or bi-racial actors and actresses. The director of the film is African American, and two high profile African-American moguls and media celebrities, Tyler Perry and Oprah Winfrey, actively promoted the film. Although the book engages with communities beyond the African-American one, the film spends very little time exploring the experiences of women from different ethnic backgrounds. Furthermore, as the film – based on a book written by the African-American poet Sapphire – centrally explores the life of an African-American girl within her community, one might logically conclude that the film is centrally concerned with and depicts experiences and happenings specific to the African-American experience, or at least one located within an urban inner-city environment. However, 15 of the film reviews analysed highlighted the film's universal nature (Sweeney 2010, Sharkey 2009, Koch 2009, Hammond 2009, Kennedy 2009, Bush 2009, Howell 2009, Longwell 2009, Vlessing 2009, Biancolli 2009, '*Precious* Based . . .' 2010, Baran 2009, Berardinelli 2009, Pols 2009, Rainer 2009), or presented the film as universal by not directly highlighting its culturally specific elements. While some suggested that the problems found in the film spoke to both an African-American experience and the experiences of those within the broader nation, others sought to move the discussion of the film away from such a focus altogether.

Of these 15 texts, three articles link the problems depicted in the film to wider social issues in the public sphere (i.e. welfare, medical and educational systems), seven linked the conflicts in the film to issues at home (i.e. in the private sphere), three primarily focused on issues at home, while at times gesturing to issues in society, and two engaged in neither of these debates, instead of focusing on the film's production and potential Oscar success. The topics that are covered when moving a discussion of the film beyond the African-American community were as follows: (1) a contemplation of incest or HIV in various communities, (2) the association of *Precious* with films that focus on other ethnicities, (3) references to the state of all poor communities regardless of ethnicity, (4) the assertion that the story is universal, (5) the claim that the film's content relates to women across different ethnic groups, (6) the opinion that the film speaks to the American dream generally and (7) a consideration of teen pregnancy. In making comparisons between different groups of people without accounting for the differences that result from the African-American experience and heritage in the United States, these reviews and articles mask and erase the very specific circumstances that have led to the mistreatment and neglect of the African-American community. To unpack how the universalising discourse found in these 15 articles is functioning, I will consider very briefly its role in the promotion of the film and highlight the way it speaks to the colour-blind discourses that were dominant in the West during the film's production and reception.

In some ways, the texts' incorporations of a universalising discourse are not surprising. After all, targeting and attracting the largest possible audience can be an important strategy for films that wish to maximise their potential box office success. Thus, when articles make comments like, 'It's an improbable success story that hits you in the gut and strikes a universal chord of recognition for anyone – black, white, or purple' (Hammond 2009: 37), it is tempting to read this type of language as a reflection of the film's efforts to target a large demographic to maximise profits; or as a reflection of the reviewer's attempt to encourage as many people as possible to see a film they highly rate or, perhaps, have a financial interest in promoting. Yet there is a problem with reading these types of comments simply within the context of box office or advertising discourses. If we instead explore the agenda-setting function of these texts in relation to broader socio-cultural discussions of race in the West, I argue that what we will find is a struggle to address the depictions of structural racism in and the racial stereotyping perpetuated by the film, as *Precious* is interpreted through and informed by a colour-blind lens. To explain how these film reviews engage with the colour-blind discourses that circulated and were perpetuated during the film's production and release, I will first outline what colour-blind racism is.

Colour-blind racism is 'a post-civil rights era ideological iteration of racism in which proponents assert that race no longer impacts inequality' (Anderson and Grether 2017: 189). This ideology gained renewed dominance in the run-up to and following Obama's election, as the election of an African American, or rather bi-racial, president was seen as a 'transformative cultural moment that many deemed postracial' (Turner and Nilsen 2019: 4). Despite the continued regressive stereotyping of racial groups in America, including African Americans, and the large-scale racial inequalities found in the country, colour-blind racism functions as 'a contemporary set of beliefs that posit that racism is a thing of the past and that race and racism do not and should not play an important role in current social and economic realities'(ibid.). As Turner and Nilsen argue, the celebration of a multicultural society in neo-liberal media draws attention away from 'the systemic and institutionalized racism [that] impact[s] . . . minority communities' (ibid.).

For Turner and Nilsen, colour-blind racism consists of five central beliefs: (1) 'most people do not even notice race anymore', (2) racial equality has been largely achieved, (3) individual or group-level shortcomings rather than structural shortcomings are the common cause of continued racial inequality, (4) 'most people do not care about racial difference' and (5) because of these social changes, institutional remedies to address persistent racial inequalities are not required (ibid.). Of course, in contemporary times the myths of colour-blind racism are more easily identified, as one can see how the Black Lives Matter movement and Donald Trump's presidency have brought to the surface the explicit and systemic racism that colour-blind racism sought to mask for many years. So while many of these articles and reviews, written in the late 2000s, may not have consciously set out to engage with colour-blind racism, in unpacking the universalising discourses found in these articles, it becomes clear that these five central beliefs at the heart of colour-blind racism find resonance with the assertions made by those writing about or seeking to promote *Precious*. My analysis in the following contemplates the ways these articles engage with the five central beliefs of colour-blind racism and how they move a discussion of *Precious* away from a discussion of the African-American culture and experiences depicted in the film.

Of the 15 articles that engage with a universalising discourse, only one article directly addresses the African-American community in any material way. The article, written for *The Lancet* by Sweeney (2010), is titled 'A Precious and Painful Life'. It reflects on the film's plot by discussing the social problems that lead to HIV transmission in America. The author discusses her experiences as an African-American woman and medical practitioner in an urban centre, who has had patients like Precious. She states, 'For those of us who work in inner cities, it is far too common for black children to be written-off – the expectation is for them to fail and when they do, sadly this is just accepted' (189). She argues that the increasing number of young Black women with HIV is a growing concern and highlights that 'a black woman is 21 times more likely to be HIV positive than a non-Hispanic white woman' and that 'AIDS is the leading cause of death among U.S. black women age 25–44 years' (ibid.) Yet, while these issues within the African-American community are highlighted, she does little to explore the systemic racism that underlines the spread of the disease. She does point to the system as being part of the problem by stating 'that HIV is the manifestation of a myriad of social problems with a medical outcome', and questions why Precious' grandmother, social worker, hospital staff and school did not seek to intervene, but ultimately she draws her strongest critique back to the women Precious' mother represents (ibid.). As she writes:

> Yet, as an African-American woman myself, I wonder how the quest for quenching pain or the zeal for sexual pleasure can be such a powerful force for some women that they will put their own lives and those of their children in jeopardy by engaging in risky sex. There are, I would suggest, women like Precious's mother who are so invested in having someone 'who's going to love me, who's going to make me feel good' that they are unable to fulfill their role as their children's nurturer and protector.
>
> (190)

From this perspective, it seems that while institutional systems may help to mitigate existing problems in the homes of some Black Americans, the source of the problem is the 'selfish' African-American woman (no mention of her lover/partner and his role in the whole affair). In focusing so strongly on the shortcomings of mothers, Sweeney seems to overlook, or at least downplay, the institutional racism that facilitates the spread of the disease. Writing in 2009 Watkins-Hayes et al. note that although Blacks made up 12% of the population in the United States, they made up 46% of the population living with HIV and 45% of new yearly infections (2009: 230). They also cite The Centre for Disease control as a source to state that the biggest demographic factor for heterosexuals living with HIV in an inner-city environment was poverty (ibid). They go on to argue:

> the AIDS epidemic in poor Black urban neighborhoods marks a deadly convergence of race, poverty, and place that exposes residents to 'limited health care access, which can reduce utilization of HIV testing and prevention services; substance abuse, which can increase sexual risk behavior; and high rates of incarceration, which can disrupt the stability of relationships.
>
> (ibid.)

While these factors point to systemic racism and deficiencies in institutional resources, and while the film highlights some of the shortcomings of these institutions, Sweeney's review to some degree shies away from these factors.

Although Sweeney addresses the film in relation to the African-American community, after each reference to this community, she extends her discussion to other groups. For example, following her argument that Black children are often written-off, she states that 'the events dramatized in *Precious* are relevant in other communities that face similar obstacles and challenges. As commonly occurs, this mother brutalizes her child and watches while her man sexually abuses their child and still blames the victim' (Sweeney 2009: 189). Sweeney reminds the reader that this problem extends beyond the African-American community but fails to highlight the way that these problems stem out of different cultural, institutional, racial and historical experiences. She roots the problem with the mother and makes the conversation about individuals rather than wider social systems and structures. She also sees the individual as central to the resolution of the issues raised in *Precious* when she points out that 'Stories like *Precious* do happen in the real world, often in oppressed communities where assistance from one person can be the beginning of turning a horrific situation around' (190). Here one is reminded that this is a wider spread problem and one fixed by individual agency rather than the address of systemic racism.

It would be simple to claim that Sweeney's analysis reflects how colour-blind racism promotes the notion that individual or group-level shortcomings, rather than structural deficiencies, result in disadvantages within a community. Yet Sweeney's review also speaks to concerns within the African-American community about representation. This becomes clear when she writes, 'There are those in the African-American community who have criticised *Precious* because they feel it reinforces the stereotype of "the Black welfare Queen"; commentators have objected to the way the film demeans African-American people who live in deprived urban communities' (189). Following this acknowledgement, she highlights that the film's representations, in her experience, are relevant to other communities that face similar challenges. As a limited number of films produced each year represent the Black community, there is a concern about the burden of representation within these communities. This concern stems from the understanding that these limited representations of an otherwise broad and diverse group of people provide one of the few spaces for others to be exposed to and gain insight into the lives of African Americans, real or imagined. Sweeney's attempt to broaden the film to a larger set of ethnic, racial and 'othered' groups might simply be a means to speak to this burden of representation and to situate the abuses depicted in the film as a broader problem in the United States. Regardless, by not highlighting the systemic racism that is unique to African-American life, by not challenging the film's depiction of 'the Black welfare Queen' and by centrally blaming mothers, Sweeney seems to mirror a colour-blind rhetoric that fails to see the systems of disadvantage that lead to the abuse and HIV transmission depicted in the film.

While Sweeney's piece is at times problematic, it at least considers the African-American community and experience in relation to the film. Most of the other 14 reviews only acknowledge the film's engagement with race passingly by mentioning that Precious is African American, Black or from Harlem; through the use of a picture from the film; by naming the actors and director, often without mentioning their race; by highlighting Tyler Perry's and Oprah Winfrey's promotion of the film; through brief references to a Black audience (often in line with a White audience); or through passing references to Black icons such as Shirley Chisholm or Toni Morrison.

Of the remaining 14 articles/reviews that adopt a universalising discourse, Koch (2009) and Sharkey (2009) highlight the shortcomings of the social system and point towards some systemic failings. Koch questions how society and the education system might address the abuse depicted in the film and admits that 'Clearly, however, we are not doing enough' (2009), while Sharkey highlights that 'There is no safety net for Precious – her family, social services and the educational system have all failed her' (2009). Although it might appear that Koch and Sharkey are moving away from the notion that it is individual or group-level shortcomings rather than structural problems that result in disadvantages within a community, they do not actually seek to explore how the events depicted in *Precious* reflect a myriad of social ills that are directly informed by the systemic racism that puts Black people at a disadvantage in the United States. Initially, it appears that Koch will make this distinction when he quotes from The National Center for Victims of Crimes and suggests that 'statistics [on incest] may be significantly low because they are based primarily on accounts of white, middle-class women and may not adequately represent low-income and minority women' (ibid.). Although this quote opens the space for Koch to discuss the reasons that low-income and minority women are underrepresented in the national statistics, the racial inequalities that the film gestures towards or how Precious represents one of these underrepresented women, Koch instead argues that 'This film concerns problems affecting both blacks and whites and should be seen by every racial group in the country' (ibid.). His reference to The National Center for Victims of Crimes serves to highlight that White middle-class women are also victims of incest. While Koch is right that incest and abuse take shape in all communities, he fails to give insight into how this type of abuse, and the support provided to the abused, takes shape and evolves in different communities. He also fails to address the quote's suggestion that the voices of abused low-income and minority women are silenced, which seems odd when reviewing a film that is seeking to give voice to a character who comes from a low-income family and represents a minority group in the United States.

Similarly, while Sharkey (2009) highlights the issue of poverty within the United States, the communities affected by this issue are framed in class-based terms, rather than in racialised terms. In this way, the child that Sharkey discusses is universalised as the divisions of race are masked. More specifically, she refers to 'the world of America's underclass' and argues that 'In a no-child-left-behind world, Precious was lost long before she could be left' (ibid.). In the first instance, Sharkey points to a disadvantaged population rooted in poverty. This focus on poverty is reaffirmed in her reference to the no-child-left-behind federal law that states that all poor children should be given extra support in schools. In other words, she makes reference to a rhetoric that addresses children united by poverty but not one unified by race. In this way, she downplays the racial dimensions of Precious' treatment within the education system, medical system, the welfare system and within the family. In fact, she makes little effort to discuss race in her review. Although she names the film's actors, actresses, director and screenwriter, highlights the film's Harlem setting and references Sapphire's book, for those who might be unfamiliar with them, the most Sharkey does to directly draw the reader's attention to race is when she describes Precious as a 'Pregnant black Harlem teen' (ibid.) at the start of the review.

In many ways, both these reviews break from the conventions of colour-blind racism as they highlight structural shortcomings and suggest that social change is needed. However, these assertions are not rooted in race. Instead, race is seemingly not noticed or not considered an important feature in which to interpret Precious' story. Koch's and Sharkey's reviews suggest that race is not a central problem and that the problems depicted are shared and equal across races. The implication is that while a social address is needed, it does not need to account for race.

Where Koch and Sharkey focus on the shortcomings of the American social system, Bush (2009) highlights the power of these social systems to address problems within the home. She writes:

> There are kids like Precious everywhere. Each day we walk by them: young boys and girls whose home lives are dark secrets. They are often abused or neglected, and seldom read to or given homework help. Without the skills they need to lead a productive life, the chances are good they will continue the cycle of poverty and illiteracy. But if young people can read and write, they are less likely to drop out of school, turn to drugs and violence, get pregnant or depend on welfare. There is not one child in America who wants that life.
>
> (2009: 16)

Bush builds on this consideration of the home to draw attention to how the film depicts education as a means to overcome issues in the home and reduce an individual's future reliance on the state. In her celebration of the power of education, she ignores the systemic problems the film points towards, such as the neglect of a school that failed to report or investigate

Precious' first pregnancy at the age of 12, which expelled her at the age of 16 because of her second pregnancy, and which showed little concern for her physical and mental welfare or the welfare of her children. Bush does not address the film's depiction of Precious as illiterate, despite her enrolment in school. Nor does she remark on the representation of a social worker, who fails to have her removed from an abusive situation. Instead, literacy becomes the solution to a problem that Bush singularly roots in the abusive and neglectful home.

In some ways this focus is unsurprising. The film promotes literacy as central to Precious's transformation. Furthermore, as a former First Lady (wife of 41st U.S. President George H.W. Bush, 1989–1993) and the founder of the Barbara Bush Foundation of Family Literacy, Bush's focus on the value of literacy is expected. For her, this movie becomes a 'call to action' in the promotion of literacy in the United States. These motivating factors see Bush, like Koch and Sharkey, ask for a structural address to a social problem, namely through the promotion of literacy. However, in not accounting for the broader institutional failings the film gestures towards, no matter how fleetingly, Bush turns a blind eye to the racial dimensions that characterise these failings.

Instead, she universalises the problems the film depicts by referring to children broadly. She only makes reference to race twice, once when she identifies Precious as an African-American teenager and once when she refers to her screening of the film where 'folks of just about every ethnic and economic background' attended. In highlighting the diversity of the audience and by generalising the problem to all abused and neglected children, the review shifts the focus away from an African-American experience. It is thus unsurprising that her solution does not seek to provide institutional remedies to persistent racial inequalities in the education system.

The reviews and articles explored so far have considered the social calling of this film, albeit in non-racialised terms. In contrast, '*Precious* Based . . .' (2010) and Kennedy (2009) both root the abuse the film depicts in family dysfunction and actively distance the film from a society-focused discourse. Writing for *Timeout*, the reviewer of '*Precious* Based . . .', for instance, states, 'It's a film that acknowledges poverty and inequality while refusing to believe that people can't escape from their grip. It's a truly American movie. Its realism is social – not socialist' (2010). The article goes on to say that 'It's a film full of life and love, well-meaning and, judging by the reaction in the U.S., a genuine and important phenomenon that says act – don't dwell – on your dreams. A genuine Obama-era movie, then' (ibid.). The review, while acknowledging the film's depiction of poverty and inequality, reaffirms to the reader that *Precious* is not asking us to take action or to see these issues as a systemic problem that needs a socialist (read institutional) solution. Instead, readers are invited to see the film as a demonstration of the American dream, of one's ability to rise above their circumstances through hard work and determination.

Further, the critic's reference to the film as an Obama-era movie calls upon the discourses around Obama's presidency as marking a post-racial society. The critic invites readers to see Precious' coming-of-age as her ability to rise above difficult circumstances like poverty, but not seemingly race, to achieve her dream. Indeed, the *Timeout* critic's alignment of the film with the Obama era serves to reinforce that the film is not exploring a character struggling with the racial inequalities of previous generations but is instead embodying the equality that Obama symbolised. Of course, this seems an odd conclusion, considering that at the end of the film Precious has yet to finish high school, she is on welfare, she is HIV positive, she has two children to care for and she is living in a halfway house. While in the closing scene Precious outlines what she plans to achieve in the future, her goals are likely unattainable because of her illness, not to mention because of the other social factors working against her. By inviting the reader not to view the film as a socialist call to action, the reviewer closes down a reading of the social and institutional failings that haunt this film. Instead, in positioning the film as an American Dream narrative, the review suggests that it is the individual rather than the society's responsibility to overcome the poverty the film presents. As commonly seen in colour-blind racism, the author moves the discussion away from that of the institutional remedies that might address persistent racial inequalities or inequalities at all.

Unlike '*Precious* Based . . .', Kennedy begins by highlighting the film's engagement with social issues when she proclaims that 'Lee Daniels' astounding second feature is, after all, the pained saga of a child shaped by abuse – sexual, emotional and, yes, socioeconomic' (2009). While she does little to really examine the socioeconomic abuse she refers to, Kennedy highlights that 'there is something obscene in a wealthy nation's children living in neglect' (ibid.). This assertion might lead one to believe that her review positions the film as a call for a social address of poverty. However, like the reviewer for *Timeout*, Kennedy does not move in this direction and quickly underlines that '"Precious" isn't a sociological diatribe. And its story of abuse isn't particular to poor folk' (ibid.). She accepts that the film is 'graphic' but does not perceive it as 'poverty porn'. Her work often seems to contradict itself. For example, she recognises poverty as a contributing factor in Precious' abuse, yet she universalises the problems the film explores by extending them beyond poorer communities. She also dismisses critics who suggest that the film is stereotypical in its depiction of poorer communities. In this way, she neither acknowledges the activism or the stereotyping in the film. Regardless of this, what is interesting for the purposes of this chapter is that the reviewer only engages with race passingly, despite being a Black woman herself. Race is highlighted through references to Harlem, the use of a screenshot from the film, references to actors and directors (without reference to their race) and passing references to Shirley Chisholm and Toni Morrison. So while the racial dimensions of the film haunt Kennedy's review, she does not seek to engage with them. The review invites readers to interpret the film primarily as a story of abuse, with some ties to poverty. As she argues that these are experiences that are felt across communities and that the film isn't a 'sociological diatribe', she invites her readers to interpret the film as one that depicts individual short-comings and one that does not invite engagement with societal concerns.

Writing specifically about colour-blindness, Doane argues that it enables society to 'deny the impact of racism' (2019: 16). By not acknowledging racism, she concludes, a social system 'that disproportionately benefits whites' continues to be upheld as the norm (ibid.). Doane suggests that this imbalance is upheld because colour-blindness becomes a political tool to 'attack affirmative action, school desegregation and other social programs and policies that are designed to remedy racial inequality or are perceived, such as public assistance, food stamps, or housing assistance, primarily to benefit communities of color' (ibid.). Read against this argument, it is clear that '*Precious* Based . . .' (2010) and Kennedy (2009) subtly reinforce a racial imbalance found in the United States and in the West more broadly in the 2000s by labelling the abuse depicted in the film as universal, by sug-gesting that the film frames the 'American dream' as realisable for all and by dismissing the idea that the film is promoting social action.

Some of the reviews (Howell 2009, Longwell 2009, Hammond 2009) actively sought to deny the impact of racism by inviting their audiences to read the film beyond the African-American community. A clear example of this is seen in Howell's review for *The Star*. He writes:

> Does it [*Precious*] unfairly demonize the black urban experience? Not according to Oprah Winfrey and Tyler Perry, who signed on as produc-ers and who have boosted the film at every turn. They understand, as should we, that it's wrong to look at *Precious* strictly in terms of race. It's not just about being black. It's about being human, and that's the most relentless thing of all.
>
> (Howell 2009)

Howell dismisses the idea that the film stereotypically depicts the Black urban community and, in this way, challenges voices within the African-American community that have criticised the film for reductively represent-ing this community. Then, drawing on two authoritative figures (Winfrey and Perry) from the Black community to further counter these dissonant

Black voices, he suggests that the reader should not singularly read the film in terms of race. Instead, he invites the reader to universalise the story to a broader community and asks that they overlook the specific racial conditions that informed Precious' abuse in the film. In telling the reader that 'it's wrong to look at *Precious* strictly in terms of race' and by suggesting that the film is about 'being human', he shuts down conversations of race and suggests that equality should be approached in terms of a human (rather than racial/cultural) experience.

In their discussion of colour-blind racism, Turner and Nilsen suggest that it speaks to the 'ideal that claims race doesn't matter – that, ultimately, we are all the same'. They argue that 'there is a level of comfort in the act of imagining an America where race and color do not play an active role in the lives of anyone – despite almost daily evidence to the contrary' (2019: 4). Howell's remarks mirror the way that colour-blind discourses suggest that there are no racial differences as equality has been achieved. Howell also invites his readers to ignore voices from the Black community that draw attention to either the stereotypical depictions found in the film or the film's address of structural racism. While reviewers such as Longwell (2009) and Hammond (2009) are not so forceful in their endeavours to highlight the universality of the film, they nonetheless also seek to draw the focus away from the Black community. In so doing they reflect the idea that race does not matter and reaffirm this act of imagining the United States as a place where race and colour, in the words of Turner and Nilsen, 'don't play an active role' (2019: 4).

From these few close readings of some of the 15 reviews and articles identified, it is clear that these writers have struggled to address a film that is rooted in race, opting instead for a universalising discourse. The complexity of the film, its problematic depictions of the urban Black community and its consideration of the institutional support (un)available to Precious are to a large extent papered over by these reviews and articles as they connect the film to a broader audience and a universal subject. These reviews reflect Turner and Nilsen's findings that colour-blind racism is a discursive framework found in mainstream, neoliberal media, that celebrates a multi-cultural society while 'disregarding the systemic and institutionalised racism impacting minority communities' (ibid.). The celebration of the film's depiction of a 'universal' story becomes a red herring. It serves to protect White privilege by denying the existence of racial inequality and by extension the need for institutional remedies to address persistent racial problems.

Highlighting race

On the other hand, 15 of the articles reviewed for this chapter addressed race directly (Kelley 2009, Morris 2009, Rodriguez 2009, Gleiberman

2009, 'Escaping from Hell . . .' 2009, Orr 2009, Lumenick 2009, Ross 2010, Mondello 2009, Lane 2009, Bradshaw 2010, Stevens 2009, Edelstein 2009, Schuker 2009, Johnson 2009). Two articles sought to consider the African-American community's response to the film in relation to discourses of victimhood, and five aimed to draw attention to the continued racism in America and the under-representation of poor African-American girls on screen. Six reviews highlighted the stereotypes about the African-American community that were seemingly perpetuated by the film, while another six reflected on the community in a negative way through the use of mild/implicit to strong/explicit racist statements.

Considering African Americans' varied response to the film, Kelley (2009) gives that clearest account of the level of division that permeated their views:

> *Precious* is not an easy movie to watch, and there are people in the black community who wish that you wouldn't. They insist that it is yet another stereotypical demonizing representation of black people. The other camp, however, is thrilled to see a depiction of a young African-American woman that while heartbreaking, is a portrait of the black experience that has been overlooked on the sunny horizon that stretches from *The Cosby Show* to *House of Payne*.
>
> (Kelley 2009: 61)

What is at the heart of the disagreement Kelley highlights is a contrasting view on the burden of representation. Shohat and Stam state that as colonised people are often treated as '"all the same," any negative behavior by any member of the oppressed community is instantly generalized as typical, as pointing to a perpetual backsliding toward some presumed negative essence' (2014: 184). They argue that while negative stereotypes are generally hurtful to any community, some communities, such as majority group communities, have 'the social power to combat and resist them' (183). In contrast, when minority groups are stereotyped, they 'participate in a continuum of prejudicial social policy and actual violence against disempowered people, placing the very body of the accused in jeopardy' (ibid.). Kelley's reflection on how some within the African-American community see this film as promoting stereotypical and demonising representations of Black people highlights their fear that *Precious* will negatively impact a community that, despite its breadth and diversity, is often treated as 'all the same' and has been historically persecuted because of the promotion of regressive stereotypes.

In contrast with this view are those who, as Kelley suggests, see *Precious* as giving voice to an often-overlooked member of the African-American community. The high rates of African-American inner-city poverty and HIV contraction in the 1980s to the present day would suggest that aspects of the film reflect and speak to experiences within some segments of that community. Furthermore, as African-American girlhood is rarely depicted, there is truth in the assertion that the film represents a voice that is largely unheard. Regardless, the tension between these two perspectives highlights how *Precious* brings to light the difficulty of exploring the diversity of experience within this community, when negative stereotypes continue to overshadow and inform the treatment of African Americans at the time of the film's release. So while the burden of representation is not a theme the film explores directly, it nonetheless becomes entrenched in debates sur-rounding it.

The concerns about whether the film reflects reality or promotes stereo-types about the African-American community are mobilised in many of the reviews that directly address the film's depiction of that community or African-American girlhood more specifically. We are reminded by review-ers like Morris, of how rare depictions of poor African-American girlhood is when he writes that the film '. . . enters the mind and feelings of a young black girl. That's a feat so rare some moviegoers might want to bring a pass-port' (2009). Reviewers like Morris, Rodriguez (2009), Gleiberman (2009) and the author of 'Escaping from Hell . . .' seek to celebrate how the film draws our attention to 'America's internal war with its own racism' ('Escap-ing from Hell . . .' 2009: 87); highlight how the legacy of racism still haunts and informs the African-American community (Gleiberman 2009); and use important figures within the African-American community, like Susan Tay-lor, who have sought to show young African-American girls and women that they are beautiful (Morris 2009).

Yet, despite the celebratory tone these reviews sometimes take in their assessment of the film, they do not shy away from engaging with issues relating to stereotypes. For instance, Morris gives pause for thought about the film's stereotypical depictions of the African-American community, especially when he highlights how all Precious' saviours are light-skinned (2009), which points to what Kelley tellingly labels 'the old problem of com-plexion' (2009). Yet Morris seems to undermine the problematic nature of this depiction when he says that 'Daniels seems loosely aware of it. When Mary arrives to make her unfathomable apology to Precious, her face is coated with white powder. Who is she trying to fool?' (2009). Morris seems to rationalise the film's problematic casting, by suggesting that the direc-tor is conscious of skin tone and has sought to lighten Mo'Nique's skin so that the 'bad guy', Mary, is not stereotypically dark in complexion. While this is implied by Morris' statement, the reviewer makes no effort to fully reflect on the anti-colourist statement he infers the director is making by altering Mary's skin tone (if indeed this is the case, as it is not clear to me that Mo'Nique is wearing 'white powder' when she, like Mary, seeks to rec-oncile with Precious) (see Figure 4.1). Regardless of whether she was or was not wearing white powder, Morris' question of 'Who is she trying to fool?' seems to imply that the audience could not be tricked into thinking that she has lighter skin and by extension is a 'good' character. Morris' rejection of the actress's light skin masquerade sees him reaffirm skin tone racism.

Morris is not alone in highlighting stereotypical aspects of the film, only to reassure the audience that an appropriate balance has been struck. Both Orr (2009) and Lumenick (2009) make similar suggestions. Orr highlights the film's engagement with skin tone prejudice when he states that 'There are moments, too, when acknowledging reality and stooping to stereotype are not so far apart' (2009). However, ultimately, he concludes that 'while the film manages, to my eye, to hew to the proper side of this line, not everyone may agree' (ibid.). For Orr, while the film's engagement with skin-colour prejudice is questionable, for the most part the film avoids 'stooping to stereotype[s]' (ibid.) His recognition that 'not everyone may agree' goes further than Morris (2009) in suggesting that the film might not be as pro-gressive or realistic in its depiction of the African-American community. However, unlike Morris, Orr ultimately undermines the problematic nature of the film's stereotypical depictions through the assertion that for him the film stays on 'the proper side of this line' (2009).

Rather than skin tone, Lumenick is primarily concerned with how the film was marketed around the politics of victimhood, a narrative deriving from protest novels that see 'African Americans become trapped by their own

Figure 4.1 Mary when she attends the welfare office to reconnect with Precious

victimhood, lacking identity without their suffering and incapable of ame-liorating their situation' (Fierce 2015: 51). Yet, despite the marketing for the film within the politics of victimhood and the fact that, for Lumenick, the film 'occasionally succumbs to melodramatic excess and stereotype' (2009), Lumenick tells his readers that they should miss this film 'at [their] peril' (ibid.). His insistence that the reader should see the film, despite its 'melo-dramatic excess and stereotype', suggests that the film's success overshad-ows any concerns one might have over its stereotypical depictions (ibid.).

Despite celebrating the film and/or questioning its stereotypical quali-ties, some of these reviews also make use, at varying degrees, of racist dis-courses. Morris, for example, uses questionable language. He writes, 'the movie looks into this girl's wide, brown face and her bleak little life, and sees, despite everything, a reason to live' (2009). The statement here sug-gests that both her bleak life and the colour of her skin are reasons not to live and that she struggles to survive despite what Morris frames as obvious limitations. It is possible that the reviewer was simply reflecting on how her skin colour creates additional challenges for her. However, as the review never addresses the film's depiction of systemic racism, Morris' language seems to align with a racist discourse around skin colour. Similarly, his discussion of colour tone, as detailed previously, reaffirms racialised stereo-types around light and dark skin.

Ross (2010) also uses racist language. Her review suggests that 'the film dissatisfies as much as it satisfies' before stating, 'Precious is not just black but *very* black; so black she almost shines blue'. While the racist nature of this description is itself apparent, the framing of Precious' dark skin as a point of criticism is reaffirmed as it is paired with the reviewer's assertion that Precious' 'face is so big and heavy all normal expression is limited' (ibid.). Ross thus invites her readers to find fault with Precious' skin colour in the same way that she invites them to find fault with her weight.

While Ross' comments about skin colour are easy to identify as racist, I would argue that her criticism of weight also has racist origins. She is not alone in her critique of Precious' weight. Mondello writes, 'her face so full it seems incapable of expression' (2009); Lane states, 'She is grimly overweight, her face so filled out that the play of normal expression seems restricted; yet Sidibe does wonders with that sad limitation, and we learn to spot the flare of anger in her eyes' (2009); while Bradshaw says:

> Precious can't help the racism that may be coming her way on account of the colour of her skin, or the sexist jibes from nasty guys on street corners, and she certainly can't help the rape and abuse she suffered. But how about being fat? Isn't it bad for her? Aren't any of these car-ing teachers going to mention heart disease, or talk to Precious about

overeating as addiction, or as the symptom of abuse? I had the uneasy
sense that her body mass index was being tacitly treated as part of her
cultural identity, and not to be questioned.

(2010)

He goes on to complain that 'The beautiful, inspirational teacher of hers
(who is naturally as thin as a rake) actually encourages Precious to eat some
more when she is round at her comfortable, middle-class professional home –
because she feels hungry!' (ibid.). While on the surface these comments may
not appear to be race related, and one might argue that they are instead tied
to fat shaming discourses, obesity has long been a racialised stereotype connected to the African-American woman. Sanders draws on Roberts (1997: 13)
and hooks (1981: 84) to remind us of mythic African-American stereotypes
such as the mammy, 'an obedient domestic servant, [who was] invariably
portrayed as "rotund" or "preferably obese"' (2019: 296). This representation
was later combined with the figure of the jezebel ('a deviant black female
[hyper] sexuality' [ibid.]), and the figure of the Black matriarch (who is
depicted as a 'working mother who fails to model deferent femininity for her
children, lacks time to give them attention and care, and is thus responsible
for their failure to succeed' [ibid.]) to create 'the controlling image of the
welfare queen' (ibid.). As obesity is connected to these negative, racist and
destructive stereotypes of Black womanhood, it becomes a sight to articulate
racial tensions, even when race is not specifically mentioned.

Further, in recent years, as discourses around obesity have been shaped
by neoliberal values, health has been reframed as a personal responsibility.
Bodies that do not conform to the ideals of body maintenance and low BMIs
are seen to reflect undisciplined bodies, ones that lack the ability of restraint
or hard work (Sanders 2019: 291). When one is perceived as failing to take
personal responsibility for their health and to conform to the notion that
they have a duty to stay well, that individual's weight becomes subjected
to a cultural means of discrimination, a form of prejudice that reflects how
the African-American 'welfare mother' has been discriminated against as a
figure of excess, as lazy and as a drain on society. Thus, while the criticism
of Precious' weight is at times framed in terms of her health (though more
often than not it is framed in regard to her beauty or ability to be expressive as an actress), this criticism becomes a means to suggest that her body,
or more specifically the body of the actress, reflects an undisciplined and
thus out of control body – the out-of-control body of the African-American
woman, as she has long been framed.

Tied to this discussion of weight is the privileging of White European
beauty. As Shaw argues, the slim European body has long been privileged
in the West, with its 'high cheekbones, straight noses, relatively thin lips,

and of course, slender bodies' (2006: 3), not to mention fine hair. European beauty has often been the marker for Hollywood beauty, as the slim and refined European features were seen as more expressive than ethnic or racial characteristics. Thus, as the reviews seek to critique Precious, or rather the actress that plays her, for her full face, what they really target is her inability to conform to Western European perspectives of female beauty.

Considering Bradshaw's (2010) criticism that the film treats Precious' obesity as part of her cultural identity, it is clear that he invites his readers to think poorly of a culture that, he suggests, accepts weight issues as a cultural norm. He overlooks how the film explores the politics of food and its connection to abuse. Food within Precious' home is repeatedly connected to abuse, whether through the screen cuts between her rape and food frying on the stove, or in moments when she is either denied food and starved or force-fed food by her mother when she is full. There are only two moments in the film where food is treated as a possible source of nutrition and care. This occurs in the hospital when a nurse instructs Precious on the importance of eating healthy food and staying away from McDonalds, and when Precious' teacher encourages her to eat, without judgement and without either withholding food or forcing food upon her. Bradshaw does not consider the implications of these depictions. Instead, Precious' eating and obesity become markers of her ill-discipline, seeing her framed within neo-liberal discourses around health as well as stereotypical discourses around African-American womanhood as detailed previously.

As the criticisms of Precious are directed at her person, the conversation obscures the racial inequalities that have contributed to the high rates of obesity within the African-American community, such as poor access to health care, the limited number of grocery stores in poor communities and the availability of cheap processed and sugary food in contrast to expensive healthier options. As Sanders suggests, by charging the individual with the responsibility to keep healthy and obtain a healthy BMI, this discourse 'obscures the deep roots of racial wealth and health disparities in state policies, systematic discrimination, and structural forces' (2019: 291).

While most of the articles that explore *Precious* in relation to race are centrally concerned with whether or not the film reflects reality or stereotype, Kelley's (2009) review suggests that both these considerations overlook what is perhaps so alarming about the film. She argues that it is shocking that while the film is set in the 1980s, 'no one seems outraged that so little has changed in the inner city in more than 20 years since' (Kelley 2009). She asserts that those who celebrate the film for Precious' strength simply accept that the broken system cannot be changed but only perhaps overcome, while those who reject the film for its perpetuation of Black victimhood fail to identify the ways that structural racism has enabled the continued repression of African Americans. Rather than seeing the depiction of Precious' parents as the central tragedy of the film, she argues that they are red herrings. Instead, she roots the travesty of the film in its inability to imagine how the structural racism that has long kept African Americans in poverty and in cycles of abuse might be overcome, and in the film's inability to imagine an ending where the African-American girl does not simply rely on a helping hand but instead challenges this system to bring about real change.

In challenging those who reject and celebrate the film, Kelley's article is one of the few reviews that asks the reader to view the film in relation to structural racism and to consider how America's internal struggle with racism has limited the ability to imagine avenues for change. Considering the relationship between structural racism and colour-blind racism, Doane suggests that 'Colorblindness is also challenged by those who argue that structural and institutional racism is still a major force in American society – an ideology that might be called systemic racism consciousness . . . and which is the complete opposite of colorblindness' (2019: 18). In acknowledging the film's direct ties to the African-American community, and by asking the reader to move beyond a discussion of stereotypes to consider systemic racism, Kelley challenges the colour-blind racism found in reviews and encourages the audience to consider how the film's own positioning at times masks the racism within its own text.

Anderson and Grether tell us that 'If people continue to believe in racial stereotypes, they may begin to elevate those beliefs as explanations for racial differences rather than systemic inequalities based on race' (2017: 189). Where Kelley (2009) asks us to move beyond a consideration of African-American stereotypes, articles that focus on the film's engagement with stereotypes limit a consideration of the film to issues of representation rather than structural and imbedded forms of discrimination. Like many of the universalising texts, articles that ask us to only consider the film in terms of its representation of African Americans serve to divert attention away from the structural racism that haunts the film and which haunted American society at the time of the film's release.

Conclusion

Of the four remaining articles that have not been addressed, one examined the legal battle between The Weinstein Company and Lionsgate over distribution rights and paid no attention to the content or reception of the film (Belloni 2010); one explored the opportunities afforded to the director and some cast members following *Precious'* success at the Oscars (Kit 2010);

one highlighted the director's, producer's and cast's acceptance of their five Spirit awards at the 25th Film Independent Spirit Awards (Kilday 2010); and one discussed the film in relation to its casting, the relationship between cast members, and the relationship between the cast and the director (Kuhn 2009). Kit (2010), Kilday (2010) and Kuhn (2009) all make passing comments about race, though little time is spent considering the important role it plays in the film.

While so much more could be said about how *Precious* was received and addressed by the media, this chapter has sought to highlight the two central themes and topics of discussion that were covered by the vast majority of the film reviews and articles analysed for this chapter. What I found is that very few articles sought to address the structural racism that haunts the film. This is perhaps not surprising as colour-blind racism was dominant at the time of the film's release and a discussion of structural racism challenges the myth of equality that colour-blind racism promotes. The upholding colour-blind racism was achieved within reviews and articles through claims made about the universality of the film, or through a focus on whether the film was stereotypical or not. What this suggests is that an understanding of the film was strongly filtered through a colour-blind ideological framing. However, upholding of colour-blind racism within the reviews also suggests that the film in some ways offers itself up to a colour-blind reading. As I pointed towards in Chapter 1, the film's neoliberal framing and softened critique of the social system masks the abuse and neglect that Precious experiences outside of the home. As this abuse outside the home is rooted in structural racism, the film underplays the significance of this discrimination to the character's life. Nonetheless, though the film does not belabour the structural racism that the novel is at pains to highlight, to suggest that this critique is not there would misrepresent the film. So the underplaying and, to some degree, erasure of this structural racism occurs through the intersection between the film's storytelling and the at times willful (re)reading of the film by media critics.

Notes

1 'The 100 Best Black Movies of the 21st Century' (2018) *Rotten Tomatoes*, online, https://editorial.rottentomatoes.com/guide/best-black-movies-21st-century/.
2 *Back Stage, Boston, Denver Post, Entertainment Weekly, Hollywood Reporter, Los Angeles Times, Maclean's, Miami Herald, New Statesman, Newsweekly, New Republic, New York Magazine, New York Post, NPR, Reelviews, RollingStone, SFGATE, Slate, The Atlantic, The Christian Science Monitor, The Economist, The Guardian, The Lancet, The New Yorker, The Spectator, The Star, Time International, Time Out, Wall Street Journal,*

3 Both the figures for the budget of *Avatar* and *Precious* were obtained from their respective Internet Movie Database pages: www.imdb.com/title/tt0499549/?ref_=fn_al_tt_2 (for *Avatar*) and www.imdb.com/title/tt0929632/?ref_=fn_al_tt_1 (for *Precious*)

4 The figures for the budgets of all these films were obtained from their respective Internet Movie Database pages (www.imdb.com).

Conclusion

Precious was labelled an unlikely success story as its careful distribution attracted Hollywood's attention and helped it to gain widespread success and recognition. The film was a box office hit with a worldwide theatrical gross of $63,649,529 on an estimated $10,000,000 budget and was nominated for numerous awards at the Golden Globes, the Screen Actors Guild Awards and the Academy Awards, with Mo'Nique winning a Best Supporting Actress award in all three, and Geoffrey Fletcher winning an Academy Award for Best Adapted Screenplay.[1]

However, was this surprise at the film's success within the Academy and more broadly warranted? On the one hand, the depiction of African-American girlhood, never mind depictions of poor, obese, sexually and physically abused African-American girls, on screen is a rarity. As the film is told from the first person, *Precious* literally gives voice to this often-underrepresented figure. In terms of narrative and representation, on the surface, the film seems like an unlikely fit for Hollywood. In financial terms, the film is a far cry from the Hollywood blockbuster, having neither a large budget nor the large worldwide grossing power that has come to be associated with blockbuster films. This indeed is a reminder of the film's limited popularity among movie-going audiences, and these factors do seem to position the film as an unlikely success story within a market-driven Hollywood.

Yet, despite these characteristics, it is not too surprising that *Precious* was scooped up, distributed, and ultimately promoted and celebrated by Hollywood. As I have demonstrated, the film moves away from many of the politics found in Sapphire's book and downplays the structural and systemic problems that Sapphire strongly identifies as the root of Precious' struggles. In so doing, the film engages with and opens itself up to be read within a colour-blind and neoliberal framework. While Precious does not achieve the American Dream that young people within White Western youth films often work towards and seem likely to achieve, the main character's journey is nonetheless structured within the ideals of the American Dream, as her

DOI: 10.4324/9781315545547-6

hard work, determination and struggle see her improve her life and the life of her children, though in a limited way. Daniels' efforts to lighten the film's tone soften its broader social politics. Thus, while the film visually focuses on the African-American community through its Black or bi-racial casting, Daniels removes references to African-American literature found in Sapphire's book and only fleetingly refers to the African-American politics that the author is at pains to discuss and question.

In downplaying an exploration of African-American culture, heritage and politics, the film is made accessible to a White audience who may feel put off or threatened by a narrative that exposes White privilege and the systemic racism that enables this White privilege. These alterations would also make *Precious* more palatable to Hollywood, as the film aligns itself with dominant ideologies that have enabled the White elite in Hollywood to maintain control of the industry and its profits. For these reasons, it is perhaps not surprising that *Precious* was accepted by Hollywood with open arms. As it was promoted as a film that could relate to anyone, White or Black, *Precious* to some degree becomes the mouthpiece for ideologies that serve to repress the African-American community for the benefit of the White elite and a White society. In this way, the Black director, Black cast and Black narrative become the site to naturalise and reinforce some regressive White Western values and stereotypes about the African-American community, at the same time as it also gives a voice to a segment of the African-American community that continues to struggle with poverty, HIV transmission and invisibility.

This leaves the question of where *Precious* sits among other African-American youth films produced from 2009 onwards. According to Pimentel and Sawyer, in '2009 alone, several feature films emerged from the Hollywood scene that centered on the theme of African Americans needing to rise up or be rescued from their impoverished, abusive and/or dysfunctional families and communities' (2011: 104). Pimentel and Sawyer identify *Precious* alongside films such as *The Blind Side* (Hancock, 2009) and *The Princess and the Frog* (Clements and Musker, 2009), as drawing on these themes (ibid.)[2] – although these two films are not conventional youth films but ones with a strong youth element. This trend of course does not start in 2009, nor does Pimentel and Sawyer suggest that it does. Instead, as detailed in Chapter 2, African-American youth films commonly promote the idea of youths in need of (White) middle-class uplift to escape the streets. *Precious* consequently reflects broader trends in the genre and themes found in (Hollywood) films that depict African-American youth and Black girlhood.

Since *Precious'* release, there has been an increasing number of films about African-American girlhood, including *Premature* (Green, 2019), *See You Yesterday* (Bristol, 2019), *The Hate U Give* (Tillman, 2018), *Night Comes*

On (Spiro, 2018), *A Wrinkle in Time* (DuVernay, 2018), *Deidra & Laney Rob a Train* (Freeland, 2017), *Roxanne Roxanne* (Larnell, 2017), *Beasts of the Southern Wild* (Zeitlin, 2012) and *Pariah* (Rees, 2011). With the exception of *A Wrinkle in Time*, all these girlhood films are set within poor or working-class Black communities. Like *Precious*, several films (*See You Yesterday, The Hate U Give, Deidra & Laney Rob a Train, Roxanne Roxanne, Pariah*) engage with the idea of needing to escape a dysfunctional home or a community that limits the main character's future potential. The dangers of street life and the uplift facilitated by education or music tend to feature strongly in such films. Even titles that are not focused on the need for social uplift tend to represent dysfunctional families and the ways they impact the young people's lives (*Night Comes On, Beasts of the Southern Wild*).

In addition to representations of dysfunctional homes, communities, gang violence, addiction and/or drug culture, films such as *See You Yesterday* and *The Hate U Give* focus on the dangers of police brutality. The brutality is not targeted directly towards the female characters, but rather the important men in their lives. The depictions of girlhood in these films are consequently structured around female characters' efforts to address the police violence experienced by male characters. This represents an interesting shift in films about girlhood, although, problematically, as the girls' stories revolve around men, they in some ways become secondary to their male counterparts. Furthermore, such representations overshadow the ways that Black girls and women also experience police brutality. It is interesting to note that this is a topic that is brought up in other girlhood films, such as *Premature*, though it is not the central focus of the film. Although these topics open the space to explore racism within America, films such as *The Hate U Give* have been accused of 'racial ventriloquism' (Dowie-Chin et al. 2020: 134). Like *Precious*, there are consequently questions as to whether these films are representing Black politics and voices, or whether these Black girlhood films are whitewashing these topics. As police brutality is also explored in films about adult African Americans, it would be interesting to examine whether these types of narratives play out in the same ways in films about Black adulthood and Black girlhood, or whether these age base categories make a difference to the narratives told about these characters.

Pregnancy and Black men as destabilising forces feature in *Premature, Night Comes On* and *Roxanne Roxanne*. The last one offers a particularly bleak representation of Black masculinity and street life, which the main female character must learn to escape from. In *Night Comes On,* the main character's father brutally murders her mother in front of her, yet again an example of the Black man as a violent aggressor, while *Premature* engages with the difficulties of a relationship between a young girl and an older male Black lover as well as pregnancy and abortion. Clearly, the negative connotations of Black sexuality and toxic Black masculinity continue to take shape within films about Black girlhood.

Of the films detailed previously, *Roxanne Roxanne* and *Night Comes On* are the darkest films. They are marked by the same hopelessness found in *Precious*, as the characters are controlled and exploited by abusive family members, lovers and/or communities. The characters are belittled and struggle to find their place, success and a sense of self-worth. Like Precious, they are positioned as underdogs that audiences are invited to root for. As the source of their problems largely seems to originate from the betrayal and violence of Black men and/or a dysfunctional community, like many preceding African-American youth films, these two films seemingly highlight the need for characters to rise above or escape their communities, home lives and histories, rather than invite scrutiny of the systems and structures that oppress them.

In short, since *Precious'* release there seems to be little change in the broader themes and messages found in movies about African-American girlhood. Despite the increasing number of African-American girlhood films, proportionally to other Hollywood films, relatively few movies have been produced in America. Of the films that have been made, issues of representation persist as they reproduce stereotypes, engage in racial ventriloquism or take shape within a colour-blind framing. As such, the degree in which African-American girlhood reflects, deviates from, reimagines or challenges White Western frames is a worthy avenue for future analysis. There also needs to be a consideration of how these films align with and deviate from Black feminist perspectives. Doing so will enable scholars to question whether or to what extent these characters give voice to experiences of Black girlhood. Of the films that have been produced, one trend that is worth exploring and which does not feature in *Precious* is the focus on police brutality. It would be worth considering the role police brutality plays in these girlhood films and whether these narratives provide avenues to address Black history, politics and culture. Furthermore, one might consider whether these narratives provide an avenue to explore girlhood, or whether girlhood becomes the vehicle to address broader politics of racialised violence and the Black Lives Matter movement.

It is easy to see why so many critics wished to view *Precious* as a success story for the way that it seemed to break down racial barriers to gain recognition within Hollywood and the Academy, and for the way that it gave voice to a segment of society that too often is silenced. *Precious* does these things and should be recognised for its accomplishments. However, like any text, the film is caught up in the politics of its time, and its navigation of these politics often saw the film reiterate rather than challenge stereotypes and prejudices. As the film and its reception became entwined in colour-blind discourses and neoliberal values, the structural racism and socialism explored in the novel were softened. This is not to suggest that the book is a singularly progressive text; it is not. At the same time that the book generates a nuanced understanding of African-American girlhood and the challenges systemic racism creates in the life of poor and underprivileged African-American girls, it uses and thus perpetuates stereotypes of the welfare queen and the Black man as rapist. As Mary's and Carl's roles are central to Precious' story and history, and as the film sought to be 'guided by' and 'be true' to the novel, the film was trapped by the stereotypes found in the book. The repetition of these stereotypes was thus foreseeable. However, where the book is progressive in its critique of structural racism, the film shies away from these criticisms and instead reflects the dominant values of colour-blindness and neoliberalism, which put the responsibility on individuals rather than on a wider social system. It consequently reproduces all the stereotypes found in the book, without spending a great deal of time representing the racially progressive politics that the book articulates.

Precious opens the space to question broader myths around the African-American child, youth and girl. Yet, as the film closely aligns itself with the tropes and conventions of the African-American school film, it is education, rather than racial politics, that becomes the film's central focus. This focus can be seen in its engagement with questions pertaining to genre and its critical reception. As such, while the film gives voice to an African-American girl rarely seen on screen, it does not unpack the complexities of her life – past, present and future – beyond a narrative of uplift through (middle-class and often White) education. As a result, *Precious* makes for an interesting example of youth film, one nonetheless that does not exploit its political potential.

Notes

1 The box-office figure was obtained from the film Internet Movide Database page.
2 Kathryn Linder (2012) also discusses how these themes play out in *Akeelah and the Bee* (2006).

Bibliography

Allen, R.C. and Gomery, D. (1985) *Film History: Theory and Practice*, New York: Knopf.

Anderson, A. and Grether, S. (2017) 'Reviewing the Reviews: Discussions of Race by Film Reviewers,' *Sociological Spectrum*, Vol. 37, No. 3, pp. 188–204.

Andrew, D. (1984) *Concepts in Film Theory*, Oxford: Oxford University Press.

Bailey, B. (2013) 'The Vexed History of Children and Sex,' in P. Fass (ed.) *The Routledge History of Childhood in the Western World*, Oxon: Routledge, pp. 191–210.

Baran, S. (2009) 'A "Precious" Legacy,' *Hollywood Reporter*, Vol. 412, No. 5, p. 18.

Barker, M. (2004) 'News, Reviews, Clues, Interviews and Other Ancillary Materials: A Critique and Research Proposal,' *Scope*, online, February, www.nottingham. ac.uk/scope/documents/2004/february-2004/barker.pdf.

Belloni, M. (2010) 'Lionsgate, TWC Settle on "Precious",' *Hollywood Reporter*, Vol. 414, No. 7, p. 5.

Benton, M., Dolan, M. and Zisch, R. (1997) 'Teen Films: An Annotated Bibliography,' *Journal of Popular Film and Television*, Vol. 25, No. 2, pp. 83–8.

Berardinelli, J. (2009) '*Precious* (United States, 2009),' *Reelviews Movie Reviews*, online, 3 November, www.reelviews.net/reelviews/precious.

Biancolli, A. (2009) '"Precious": Searing Look at Despair, Resilience,' *SFGate*, online, 13 November, www.sfgate.com/movies/article/Precious-Searing-look-at-despair-resilience-3281441.php.

Bode, L. (2010) 'Transitional Tastes: Teen Girls and Genre in the Critical Reception of Twilight,' *Continuum*, Vol. 24, No. 5, pp. 707–19.

Bourdieu, P. (1984) *Distinction: A Social Critique of the Judgement of Taste*, Cambridge: Harvard University Press.

Bradshaw, P. (2010) 'Precious: Based on the Novel Push by Sapphire,' *Guardian*, online, 28 January, www.theguardian.com/film/2010/jan/28/precious-review.

Brooks, W. and McNair, J. (2015) '"Combing" Through Representations of Black Girls' Hair in African American Children's Literature,' *Children's Literature in Education*, Vol. 46, No. 3, pp. 296–307.

Bruhm, S. and Hurley, N. (2004) 'Curiouser: On the Queerness of Children,' in S. Bruhm and N. Hurley (eds.) *Curiouser: On the Queerness of Children*, Minneapolis: University of Minnesota Press, pp. ix–xxxvii.

Bush, B. (2009) 'A Precious Moment,' *Newsweek*, Vol. 154, No. 24, p. 16.

Carroll, N. (1985) 'The Specificity of Media in the Arts,' *Journal of Aesthetic Education*, Vol. 19, No. 4, pp. 5–20.

Cartmell, D. and Whelehan, I. (eds.) (1999) *Adaptations: From Text to Screen, Screen to Text*, London: Routledge.

Caruth, C. (1996) *Unclaimed Experience: Trauma, Narrative, and History*, Baltimore: Johns Hopkins University Press.

Coleman, J. (2011) *The Nature of Adolescence*, New York, NY: Taylor & Francis.

Colling, S. (2017) *The Aesthetic Pleasures of Girl Teen Film*, Bloomsbury: New York.

Crawford, H. (2012) 'Acting Out: Counterliteracy Beyond the Ree(a)l,' *Black Camera: An International Film Journal*, Vol. 4, No. 1, pp. 181–91.

Cunningham, H. (1995) *Children and Childhood in Western Society Since 1500*, London: Longman.

Dagbovie-Mullins, S. (2013) 'Pigtails, Ponytails, and Getting Tail: The Infantilization and Hyper-Sexualization of African American Females in Popular Culture,' *Journal of Popular Culture*, Vol. 46, No. 4, pp. 745–71.

David, M. (2016) '"I Got Self, Pencil, and Notebook": Literacy and Maternal Desire in Sapphire's PUSH,' *Tulsa Studies in Women's Literature*, Vol. 35, No. 1, pp. 173–99.

De Silva, I. (1998) 'Consumer Selection of Motion Pictures,' in B. Litman (ed.) *The Motion Picture Mega-Industry*, Needham Heights: Allyn and Bacon, pp. 144–71.

Doane, A. (2019) 'Colorblindness: The Lens That Distorts,' in S. Turner and S. Nilsen (eds.) *The Myth of Colorblindness: Race and Ethnicity in American Cinema*, Cham: Palgrave Macmillan, pp. 13–33.

Doherty, T. (2002) *Teenagers and Teenpics: Juvenilization of American Movies*, 2nd edition, Philadelphia: Temple University Press.

Dowie-Chin, T., Cowley, M.P.S. and Worlds, M. (2020) 'Whitewashing Through Film: How Educators Can Use Critical Race Media Literacy to Analyze Hollywood's Adaptation of Angie Thomas' The Hate U Give,' *International Journal of Multicultural Education*, Vol. 21, No. 2, pp. 129–44.

'DP/30: Precious, Director/Producer Lee Daniels' (2013) DP/30: The Oral History of Hollywood, *YouTube*, online, 6 January, www.youtube.com/watch?v=9gTzi C0ejl4.

Driscoll, C. (2002) *Girls: Feminine Adolescence in Popular Culture and Cultural Theory*, New York: Columbia University Press.

Driscoll, C. (2011) *Teen Film: A Critical Introduction*, Oxford: Berg.

Dyer, R. (1997) *White: Essays on Race and Culture*, Oxon: Routledge.

Edelstein, D. (2009) 'When Push Comes to Shove,' *New York Magazine*, online, 30 October, http://nymag.com/movies/reviews/61750/index.html.

Erb, C. (1998) *Tracking King Kong: A Hollywood Icon in World Culture*, Detroit: Wayne State University Press.

'Escaping from Hell; New Cinema: Lee Daniels's "Precious"' (2009) *The Economist*, 21 November, Vol. 393, No. 8658, p. 87.

Fierce, R. (2015) 'The Exceptional N*gger: Redefining African American Identity in *Django Unchained*,' in D. Izzo (ed.) *Movies in the Age of Obama: The*

Era of Post-Racial and Neo-Racist Cinema, Lanham: Rowman and Littlefield, pp. 51–61.

Foucault, M. (1978) *The History of Sexuality*, New York, NY: Pantheon Books.

Gaudreault, A. and Marion, P. (2004) 'Transécriture and Narrative Mediatics,' in R. Stam and A. Raengo (eds.) *A Companion to Literature and Film*, Oxford: Blackwell, pp. 58–70.

Geraghty, C. (2008) *Now a Major Motion Picture: Film Adaptations of Literature and Drama*, Lanham: Rowman & Littlefield.

Gilbey, R. (2010) 'Sleazy Does It,' *New Statesman*, online, 1 February, www.newstatesman.com/film/2010/02/precious-daniels-mary-father.

Gleiberman, O. (2009) 'Precious: Based on the Novel "Push" by Sapphire,' *Entertainment Weekly*, online, 19 November, https://ew.com/article/2009/11/19/precious-based-novel-push-sapphire-2/.

Graham, S. (2019) 'Introduction,' in S. Graham (ed.) *A History of the Bildungsroman*, Cambridge: Cambridge University Press, pp. 1–9.

Grant, C. (2002) 'Recognising Billy Budd in *Beau Travail*: Epistemology and Hermeneutics of an Auteurist "Free" Adaptation,' *Screen*, Vol. 45, No. 1, pp. 57–73.

Griffin, R.A. (2014) 'Pushing into Precious: Black Women, Media Representation, and the Glare of the White Supremacist Capitalist Patriarchal Gaze,' *Critical Studies in Media Communication*, Vol. 31, No. 3, pp. 182–97.

Guerrero, E. (1993) 'Framing Blackness: The African-American Image in the Cinema of the Nineties,' *Cineaste*, Vol. 20, No. 2, pp. 24–31.

Gupta, A. (2009) 'Slumdog Colonialism: Hollywood Mines Another Culture For Raw Material, Celebrates A Box-Office Bonanza,' *Indypendent*, online, 20 March, https://indypendent.org/2009/03/slumdog-colonialism-hollywood-mines-another-culture-for-raw-material-celebrates-a-box-office-bonanza/.

Hammond, P. (2009) 'Precious: Based On the Novel Push by Sapphire,' *Back Stage*, Vol. 50, No. 45, p. 37.

Hanson, S. (2000) 'Children in Film,' in J. Mills and R. Mills (eds.) *Childhood Studies: A Reader in Perspectives of Childhood*, London: Routledge, pp. 145–59.

Heywood, C. (2001) *A History of Childhood: Children and Childhood in the West From Medieval to Modern Times*, Cambridge: Polity Press.

Hockey, J. and James, A. (1993) *Growing Up and Growing Old: Ageing and Dependency in the Life Course*, Michigan: Sage.

Holland, P. (2004) *Picturing Childhood: The Myth of the Child in Popular Imagery*, London: I.B. Tauris.

hooks, b. (1981) *Ain't I a Woman?*, Boston: South End Press.

Howell, P. (2009) '*Precious: Based on the Novel "Push" by Sapphire*–Real and Raw,' *Star*, online, 20 November, www.thestar.com/entertainment/movies/2009/11/20/precious_based_on_the_novel_push_by_sapphire_real_and_raw.html.

Hughey, M.W. (2010) 'The White Savior Film and Reviewers' Reception,' *Symbolic Interaction*, Vol. 33, No. 3, pp. 475–96.

Hughey, M. W. (2014) *The White Savior Film: Content, Critics, and Consumption*, Philadelphia: Temple University Press.

Hutcheon, L. (2006) *A Theory of Adaptation*, New York, NY: Routledge.

James, A. (2000) 'Embodied Being(s): Understanding the Self and the Body in Childhood,' in A. Prout (ed.) *The Body, Childhood and Society*, Houndmills: Macmillan, pp. 19–37.

Jancovich, M. (2001) 'Genre and the Problem of Reception: Generic Classification and Cultural Distinctions in the Promotion of *The Silence of Lambs*,' in M. Jancovich (ed.) *Horror: The Film Reader*, London: Routledge, pp. 150–61.

Jarman, M. (2012) 'Cultural Consumption and Rejection of Precious Jones: Pushing Disability into the Discussion of Sapphire's *Push* and Lee Daniels's *Precious*,' *Feminist Formations*, Vol. 24, No. 2, pp. 163–85.

Jedidi, K., Krider, R. and Weinberg, C. (1998) 'Clustering at the Movies,' *Marketing Letters*, Vol. 9, No. 4, pp. 393–405.

Johnson, B. (2009) 'The Real Reason to See "Precious",' *Maclean's*, Vol. 122, No. 45, p. 70.

Kelley, R. (2009) 'The Problem with "Precious",' *Newsweek*, Vol. 154, No. 20, p. 61.

Kennedy, L. (2009) '"Precious" Walks Through Fires of Abuse into Miracle of Empathy,' *Denver Post*, online, 18 November, www.denverpost.com/2009/11/18/precious-walks-through-fires-of-abuse-into-miracle-of-empathy.

Kilday, G. (2010) 'Call it Love on a Rooftop,' *Hollywood Reporter*, Vol. 413, No. 34, pp. 14, 22.

Kim, C. (2009) '"Slumdog Millionaire" Exploitation Exposes Cultural Imperialism,' *Liberation*, online, 5 June, www.liberationnews.org/09-06-05-slumdog-millio naire-exploitati-html/.

Kincaid, J. (1998) *Erotic Innocence: The Culture of Child Molesting*, Durham, NC: Duke University Press.

Kit, Z. (2010). 'And the Nominees Are . . .,' *Back Stage*, Vol. 51, No. 7, pp. 12–13.

Klinger, B. (1994) *Melodrama and Meaning: History, Culture, and the Films of Douglas Sirk*, Bloomington, IN: Indiana University Press.

Knopfdoubleday (2009) '*Precious: Based on the Novel Push* – Sapphire Interview,' *YouTube*, online, 9 November, www.youtube.com/watch?v=Hj5gbFecRFw.

Koch, E. (2009) 'Painfully Precious,' *The Atlantic*, online, 10 November, www.theatlantic.com/entertainment/archive/2009/11/painfully-precious/29925/.

Kokkola, L. (2013) 'Learning to Read Politically: Narratives of Hope and Narratives of Despair in *Push* by Sapphire,' *Cambridge Journal of Education*, Vol. 43, No. 3, pp. 391–405.

Kredell, B. (2018) '"Complicated Negotiations": Reception and Audience Studies into the Digital Age,' *The Anthem Handbook of Screen Theory*, London: Anthem Press pp. 71–84.

Kuhn, S. (2009) 'Family Matters,' *Back Stage*, Vol. 50, No. 48, p. 12.

Kyrölä, K. (2017) 'Feeling Bad and *Precious* (2009): Black Suffering, White Guilt, and Intercorporeal Subjectivity,' *Subjectivity*, Vol. 10, No. 3, pp. 258–75.

Lane, A. (2009) 'Making Peace,' *New Yorker*, online, 9 November, www.newyorker.com/magazine/2009/11/09/marking-peace.

Leitch, T. (2017) 'Introduction,' in T. Leitch (ed.) *The Oxford Handbook of Adaptation Studies*, Oxford: Oxford University Press, pp. 1–18.

Lerner, A. and Lerner, L. (2009) '"Precious" – Lee Daniels,' *YouTube*, online, 22 November, www.youtube.com/watch?v=-2Iwl_U_Lck.

Lewis, J. (2014) *The Road to Romance & Ruin: Teen Films and Youth Culture*, London: Routledge.

Liddell, J.L. (1999) 'Agents of Pain and Redemption in Sapphire's PUSH,' in J. Liddell and Y.B. Kemp (eds.) *Arms Akimbo: Africana Women in Contemporary Literature*, Gainesville, FL: University Press of Florida, pp. 135–46.

Linder, K.E. (2012) 'Spelling Out Racial Difference: Moving Beyond the Inspirational Discourses in Akeelah and the Bee,' in V.B. Cvetkovic and D. Olson (eds.) *Portrayals of Children in Popular Culture: Fleeting Images*, Lanham: Lexington Books, pp. 207–24.

Litman, B. and Ahn, H. (1998) 'Predicting Financial Success of Motion Pictures: The Early '90s Experience,' in B. Litman (ed.) *The Motion Picture Mega-Industry*, Needham Heights: Allyn and Bacon, pp. 172–97.

Longwell, T. (2009) 'Forged in Fire,' *Hollywood Reporter*, Vol. 412, No. 4, pp. 8–9.

Lumenick, L. (2009) '"Precious" Hope Amid the Horror,' *New York Post*, online, 6 November, http://nypost.com/2009/11/06/precious-hope-amid-the-horror/.

Maltby, R. (2007) 'How Can Cinema History Matter More?,' *Screening the Past*, No. 22, www.screeningthepast.com/issue-22-tenth-anniversary/how-can-cinema-history-matter-more/.

Maras, S. and Sutton, D. (2000) 'Medium Specificity Re-Visited,' *Convergence: The International Journal of Research into New Media Technologies*, Vol. 6, No. 2, pp. 98–113.

McCallum, R. (2021) *Screen Adaptations and the Politics of Childhood: Transforming Children's Literature into Film*, London: Palgrave Macmillan.

McCulloch, F. (2019) 'Bildungsroman for Children and Young Adults,' in S. Graham (ed.) *A History of the Bildungsroman*, Cambridge: Cambridge University Press, pp. 174–99.

McFarlane, B. (1996) *Novel to Film: An Introduction to the Theory of Adaptation*, Oxford: Oxford University Press.

McNeil, E. (2012) 'Un-"Freak"ing Black Female Self: Grotesque-Erotic Agency and Ecofeminist Unity in Sapphire's PUSH,' in E. McNeil, N. Lester, D. Fulton and L. Myles (eds.) *Sapphire's Literary Breakthrough: Erotic Literacies, Feminist Pedagogies, Environmental Justice Perspectives*, New York: Palgrave Macmillan, pp. 89–111.

McNeil, E., Lester, N., Fulton, D. and Myles, L. (2014) '"Going After Something Else" Sapphire on the Evolution of *PUSH* to *Precious* and *The Kid*,' *Callaloo*, Vol. 352, No. 2, pp. 352–7.

Meek, M. (2017). '"It Ain't for Children": "Shame-Interest" in *Precious* and *Bastard Out of Carolina*,' *Literature/Film Quarterly*, Vol. 45, No. 4, https://lfq.salisbury.edu/_issues/45_4/it_aint_for_children.html.

Michals, D. (2015) 'Shirley Chisholm,' *National Women's History Museum*, online, www.womenshistory.org/education-resources/biographies/shirley-chisholm.

Michlin, M. (2006) 'Narrative as Empowerment: *Push* and the Signifying on Prior African-American Novels on Incest,' *Études anglaises*, Vol. 59, No. 2, pp. 170–85.

Mitry, J. (1971) 'Remarks on the Problem of Cinematic Adaptation,' *Bulletin of the Midwest Modern Language Association*, Vol. 4, No. 1, pp. 1–9.

Mondello, B. (2009). 'When Life is This Hard, Stubbornness is a Virtue,' *NPR*, online, 5 November, www.npr.org/templates/story/story.php?storyId=12005815 1&t=1600077382991.

Morris, W. (2009) 'Precious: Based on the Novel "Push" by Sapphire,' *Boston*, online, 20 November, http://archive.boston.com/ae/movies/articles/2009/11/20/precious_bluntly_goes_to_a_place_rarely_seen____the_life_of_a_young_black_girl/.

Nelson, E.H. (2019) *The Breakfast Club: John Hughes, Hollywood, and the Golden Age of the Teen Film*, London: Routledge.

Olson, D. (2017) *Black Children in Hollywood Cinema: Cast in Shadow*, Cham: Palgrave Macmillan.

Orr, C. (2009) 'The Movie Review: "Precious",' *New Republic*, online, 13 November, http://newrepublic.com/article/71150/the-movie-review-precious.

Owen, G. (2019) 'Adolescence, Blackness, and the Politics of Respectability in *Monster* and *The Hate U Give*,' *The Lion and the Unicorn*, Vol. 43, No. 2, pp. 236–60.

Papalia, D.E., Olds, S.W. and Feldman, R.D. (2006) *A Child's World: Infancy Through Adolescence*, New York: McGraw-Hill.

Pimentel, C. and Sawyer, C. (2011) '*Akeelah and the Bee*: Inspirational Story of African-American Intellect and Triumph or Racist Rhetoric Served up on Another Platter?,' *Multicultural Perspectives*, Vol. 13, No. 2, pp. 100–4.

Pols, M. (2009) 'Hard-Knock Life,' *Time International*, Vol. 174, No. 19, pp. 53–4.

'*Precious* Based on the Novel "Push" by Sapphire' (2010) *Timeout*, online, 29 January, www.timeout.com/movies/precious-based-on-the-novel-push-by-sapphire-1.

Pride, R. (2009) 'America as a Second Language: Talking "Precious" Style with Lee Daniels,' *New City Film*, online, 4 November, www.newcityfilm.com/2009/11/04/america-as-a-second-language-talking-precious-style-with-lee-daniels/.

Rainer, P. (2009) 'Review: "Precious Based on the Novel Push by Sapphire",' *The Christian Science Monitor*, online, 7 November, www.csmonitor.com/The-Culture/Movies/2009/1107/p17s01-almo.html.

Ravid, A.S. (1999) 'Information, Blockbusters, and Stars: A Study of the Film Industry,' *Journal of Business*, Vol. 72, pp. 463–92.

Reid, M.A. (2000) 'New Wave Black Cinema in the 1990s,' in W.W. Dixon (ed.) *Film Genre 2000: New Critical Essays*, Albany, NY: State University of New York Press, pp. 13–28.

Roberts, D. (1997) *Killing the Black Body*, New York: Vintage.

Rodriguez, R. (2009) 'Review: "Precious: Based on the Novel Push by Sapphire",' *Miami Herald*, online, 18 November, https://miamiherald.typepad.com/reeling/2009/11/review-precious-based-on-the-novel-push-by-sapphire.html.

Ross, D. (2010). 'Mixed Blessings,' *The Spectator*, online, 30 January, www.spectator.co.uk/article/mixed-blessings-30-january-2010.

Rountree, W. (2013) 'Blues, Hope, and Disturbing Images: A Comparison of Sapphire's *Push* and the Film *Precious*,' in T. Green (ed.) *Presenting Oprah Winfrey, Her Films, and African American Literature*, New York: Palgrave Macmillan, pp. 161–78.

Rutter, M. (1980) *Changing Youth in a Changing Society: Patterns of Adolescent Development and Disorder*, London: Harvard University Press.

Sanders, R. (2019) 'The Color of Fat: Racializing Obesity, Recuperating Whiteness, and Reproducing Injustice,' *Politics, Groups, and Identities*, Vol. 7, No. 2, pp. 287–304.

Sapphire (1996) *Push*, London: Vintage Books.

Schuker, L. (2009) 'Novice Film "Angels" Took Leap of Faith With "Precious",' *Wall Street Journal*, online, 16 November, www.wsj.com/articles/SB1000142405 2748704538404574537721627768260.

Sharkey, B. (2009) 'A Light in the Darkness,' *Los Angeles Times*, online, 6 November, www.latimes.com/archives/la-xpm-2009-nov-06-et-precious6-story.html.

Shary, T. (2005) *Teen Movie American Youth on Screen*, London: Wallflower.

Shary, T. (2007) 'Introduction: Youth Culture Shock,' in T. Shary and A. Seibel (eds.) *Youth Culture in Global Cinema*, Austin, TX: University of Texas Press, pp. 1–6.

Shary, T. (2014) *Generation Multiplex: The Image of Youth in American Cinema After 1980s*, Austin, TX: University Texas Press.

Shary, T. and Seibel, A. (eds.) (2007) *Youth Culture in Global Cinema*, Austin, TX: University of Texas Press.

Shaw, A.E. (2006) *The Embodiment of Disobedience: Fat Black Women's Unruly Political Bodies*, Lanham: Lexington Books.

Sheth, N. and Bellman, E. (2009) '"Slumdog" Success Gets Mixed Reviews in India,' *Wall Street Journal*, online, 24 February, www.wsj.com/articles/SB123537861516146983.

Shohat, E. and Stam, R. (2014) *Unthinking Eurocentrism: Multiculturalism and the Media*, London: Routledge.

Smith, F. (2017) *Rethinking the Hollywood Teen Movie: Gender, Genre and Identity*, Edinburgh: Edinburgh University Press.

Sochay, S. (1994) 'Predicting the Performance of Motion Pictures,' *Journal of Media Economics*, Vol. 7, No. 4, pp. 1–20.

Speed, L. (2001) 'Moving on up: Education in Black American Youth Films,' *Journal of Popular Film and Television*, Vol. 29, No. 2, pp. 82–91.

Staiger, J. (1992) *Interpreting Films: Studies in the Historical Reception of American Cinema*, Princeton: Princeton University Press.

Stam, R. (2000) 'Beyond Fidelity: The Dialogics of Adaptation,' in J. Naremore (ed.) *Film Adaptation*, New Brunswick, NJ: Rutgers University Press, pp. 54–76.

Stapleton, L. (2004) 'Toward a New Learning System: A Freirean Reading of Sapphire's "Push",' *Women's Studies Quarterly*, Vol. 32, No. 1/2, pp. 213–23.

Stevens, D. (2009) '*Precious*: Sorry I didn't Like This Movie,' *Slate*, online, 5 November, http://slate.com/culture/2009/11/sorry-i-didn-t-like-precious.html.

Stokes, M. (2001) 'Introduction: Historical Hollywood Spectatorship,' in M. Stokes and R. Maltby (eds.) *Hollywood Spectatorship: Changing Perceptions of Cinema Audiences*, London: British Film Institute, pp. 1–16.

Sweeney, M. (2010) 'A Precious and Painful Life,' *Lancet*, Vol. 375, pp. 189–90.

Thottam, J. (2009) 'The Oscar Goes To . . .,' *Time International*, Vol. 173, No. 10, p. 52.

Travers, P. (2009) '*Precious*,' *Rolling Stone*, online, 5 November, www.rollingstone.com/movies/movie-reviews/precious-246901/.

Tropiano, S. (2006) *Rebels & Chicks: A History of Hollywood Teen Movies*, New York: Back Stage Books.

Tropiano, S. (2014) 'Foreword,' in T. Shary (ed.), *Generation Multiplex: The Image of Youth in American Cinema After 1980s*, Austin, TX: University Texas Press, pp. ix–xii.

Turner, S.E. and Nilsen, S. (2019) 'Introduction,' in S.E. Turner and S. Nilsen (eds.) *The Myth of Colorblindness: Race and Ethnicity in American Cinema*, Cham: Palgrave Macmillan, pp. 1–9.

UrbanBridgez E-Zine (2009) 'Lee Daniels – *Precious*, www.Urbanbridgez.com (Lionsgate),' *YouTube*, online, 5 November, www.youtube.com/watch?v=l7Ed183H1Ns.

Vlessing, E. (2009) '"Precious" Builds Oscar Momentum,' *Hollywood Reporter*, Vol. 411, No. 29, pp. 3, 22.

Watkins-Hayes, C., Patterson, C. and Armour, A. (2009) '*Precious*: Black Women, Neighborhood HIV/AIDS Risk, and Institutional Buffers,' *Du Bois Review: Social Science Research on Race*, Vol. 8, No. 1, pp. 229–40.

Whelehan, I. (1999) 'Adaptations: The Contemporary Dilemmas,' in D. Cartmell and I. Whelehan (eds.) *Adaptations: From Text to Screen, Screen to Text*, London: Routledge, pp. 3–20.

Index

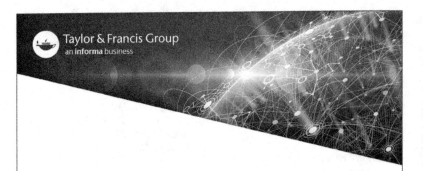

Printed in the United States
by Baker & Taylor Publisher Services